YOU ARE THE WORLD

YOU ARE THE WORLD

Creating Global Oneness

LINDA SMYTHE OLIARO & FR. BRIAN MCCORMICK

Publisher: Better Community Housing of Trenton

CONTENTS

Dedication

This book is dedicated to all the people who worked to bring Fr. Brian McCormick's mission and dreams to life - the workers, volunteers, and neighborhood people who came together, in unity, to make things happen.

And I must acknowledge the forgotten of our world, who are waiting for us to make Oneness a reality. As Fr. Brian McCormick said in a Christmas meditation in 1979:

Illuminated before us is our total tiny globe with
its billions of people, its many cultures,
its varied nations, its interrelationships
and its interdependence.
It is a beautiful and terrifying sight.

All of this demands
a new comprehension, a new way of dealing.

INTRODUCTION

Poverty Vs. the Oneness of Humanity

"What the fight against poverty really needs are men and women who live in a profoundly fraternal way and are able to accompany individuals, families, and communities on journeys of authentic human development." Pope Benedict XVI – Message for World Day of Peace 2009

This book tells the story of a how a remarkable man became a teacher and practitioner of how to live together as brothers and sisters on this planet of nearly 8 billion people. This pressing need was put forth by Pope Benedict XVI (above), as well as Pope Francis in his 2019 Encyclical, Laudato Si, *In Care of Our Common Home.*

Fr. Brian McCormick charged through life formulating and promoting soul-searching ideas about how society works and how it needs to be changed with regard to the poor. The title of this book harks back to the 1985 hit single written by Michael Jackson and Lionel Richie, "We Are the World," to raise money for famine in Africa. That title describes so well Fr. McCormick's belief that we are all one and that each person's actions affect the whole. In fact, he believes that, with God, we co-create the world we live in and, hence, our place in eternity. He reminds us, "You are not just you. You are the world."

Fr. McCormick has always been forceful about what the Church's role is and should be in forming a world conscience. His ideas are controversial, and his method of communication is often considered blunt. But it cannot be denied that his passionate beliefs and his love for God and humankind shine through to all.

At age 81, Father asked me if I could go through things he had written and collected over the years to see if there was anything there worth passing on to others. He was specifically interested in motivating people to recognize the inter-relatedness of all actions and to figure out how to live together equitably on our ever-changing planet.

In a 2015 newsletter for his Better Community Housing of Trenton ministry, he wrote:

Our shepherd, Pope Francis, asks us to look up! He asks us to see what is happening to our Common Home, the home of 7.2 billion people, on this gift of the Planet Earth where we live.

Our Holy Father reminds us that all that occurs on this planet is inter-related, and we must face and take responsibility for our man-made dilemmas – our man-made technology, economics, politics, consumerism, and commercialism.

Simultaneously and equally important, we must see the grave human tragedy that over 2 billion of our brothers and sisters are forced to live in subhuman abject poverty. This planet was created to be the home for all of us, given for us by God our Father, saved by His Son, and blessed with His Holy Spirit. In the redemptive presence of the Risen Lord, entrusted to all of us, is the creative joyful human task to make this oneness happen.

With the Good Shepherd, present with His entrusted co-shepherds, the total flock can redemptively break down the walls of enmity that separate us. We can gather together and be mutually pastured in His great flock in this one world, to be co-creators with God in the healing of the earth and the Oneness of peoples. Jesus is calling us to enhance this creative call, not with our lips, but with our hearts!

Fr. McCormick's ideas on how to make this "Oneness" a reality, and his life journey that formed the man and his ideas, take us on an interesting and thought-provoking path in this book. Part V, a compendium of his meditations, provides direct insight into his unique way of thinking and facing the world.

This book is written from my perspective, with the guidance of Fr. Brian McCormick. We hope that it will provide a basis for thought and discussion regarding how the Church and everyday people might journey together to deal with society's systemic inequities to make a better world where all recognize the Oneness we share.

Linda Smythe Oliaro
   August 1, 2023

PART I – EMBRACING THE CONCEPT OF ONENESS

Chapter 1: Formative Years

Somerville, NJ: The Encouraging Influence of Family

Although this is not a biography, it is important to give some background on how this man became the person who formulated some controversial ideas on how we must live together as one people in this world.

Perhaps not surprisingly, Brian McCormick's family (and upbringing) was his first and foremost influence and was responsible for how he came to view the world. Brian grew up in Somerville, NJ, the third of five children in a close-knit Irish Catholic family. It was 1939, and his parents ran a hotel, one of the oldest in the country. The hotel was a sort of rooming house, that served meals and had a bar and acted as a bus station and central gathering space for the town. His parents were always busy, and the children shared in the chores and interacted with the clientele. Brian was observant and questioning, responsible but independent. His responsibilities and his interactions with the diverse group of people passing through the hotel had a lasting impact on his understanding that we are all one.

One of his early memories is of going with his father to a meeting of the Tavern Owners Association and wondering why a man said that he couldn't afford to be a millionaire anymore. Brian knew some people were rich, while some struggled with life's necessities, but he didn't understand what the man meant. This is when Brian began to think about what it meant to be rich. He did not realize as a youngster that fighting to change a polarized society of Haves and Have Nots would be his life work.

Brian attended St. Joseph's Elementary School in Raritan and St. Peter's High School in New Brunswick, NJ. He struggled in school with "learning differences," in the early grades being threatened each year with being held back if he couldn't do better on his spelling. Fr. Brian was well-liked and excellent at sports, especially baseball. One of his teammates remembers that Brian would run home directly after school, complete his required chores, then run all the way back to practice. Brian was known, even then, for his dedication and strong personality – never shy to express his opinions.

Fr. Brian says that his environment helped give him a sense of the Living God at an early age. He realized few of us are exposed to the variety of people that he was at the hotel and bus station. The hotel helped him learn how we are supposed to relate to each other. His family demonstrated how everyone had to get along, in a God-centered way. They took care of people in the hotel, restaurant, and bus station, regardless of their monetary or social status. As the family dealt with the local people who didn't much care for the itinerants and weekly workers who stayed at the hotel during the week while they worked in the factories of nearby Manville, Brian began to see the separation of social classes.

Like many high school athletes, Brian had dreams of being picked up by a professional baseball team. He also had a girl he cared about very much with whom he envisioned he could settle down and have a family. But one day at confession, out of the blue, the priest told him he thought he had a vocation, a calling to the priesthood. Brian began to think and pray about this. He wondered where he could do the most good in the world. After much consideration and prayer, he decided that, as a priest, he could be more effective to a greater number of people than he could as a husband and father of several children. Thus, Brian made the difficult decision to go to seminary and see where it could take him.

College and Seminary: Eyes Open

Brian attended St. Jerome's University in Kitchener, Ontario, Canada. Once there, studying and reading remained difficult for him, but he was persistent, as well as passionate about becoming a priest and what that would mean for him. He was able to compensate for his differences and became an avid, if not a fond, reader.

Upon graduation, Brian was accepted to, and attended, Darlington Seminary in New Jersey. Always thinking outside the box, Brian tended to question the professors and express his opinions in an animated way. He began to get a reputation as a nonconformist. He had his own ideas on social justice and how the

Church should be guiding its people. For example, one of his assignments was to visit the sick. One woman he visited was very anxious about how her husband was managing at home without her. Back at seminary Brian asked if he could visit the husband. When told, no, Brian asked to contact the woman's pastor so he could take care of it, and was again told no, that was not his place. Brian told the rector he felt the visitation process was insincere. This was possibly his first view of a Church whose organization hindered Oneness.

In Brian's last year of Seminary, the rector called him to his office and suggested that he should take a break from seminary because some of his professors had some misgivings about his vocation and were uncomfortable about the way he reacted to their teachings.

After thinking and praying about his situation, Brian felt that the seminary was where God was calling him to be, and that if he "took a break" they would never let him back in. When he voiced this, the rector said he could stay if he would see a therapist. In commenting on this difficult time in his life, Fr. Brian says that he learned some interesting things about himself:

"As I think about it, I'm always a little hyperactive. I speak through this energy and enthusiasm. The doctor had me do the Rorschach ink blot test. She said, 'You're very unusual. You see everything all together all at once.' I had no idea what that meant. Years later I think I grasp its meaning for me. I see events, problems, questions all together, all at once, as I answer specific questions or set out to do

specific things... and ponder – how does everything interrelate with everything?"

This way of seeing everything all together all at once made it difficult for Brian to put things in writing in a cohesive way that made sense to others, so his writings were sometimes difficult to interpret. This was something that followed him through seminary and his priestly ministry.

Brian made it through seminary, but always remembered what the therapist said on conclusion of her sessions with him. She told him that he held and acted on deeper beliefs than many others and that that would cause him problems as he pursued his ministry. And it was true that Fr. Brian continued to firmly preach his differing views at age 40, and still at age 80 – to the bishop, other priests, and all who would listen. And he was often going against the tide.

Fr. Brian McCormick was ultimately ordained as a parish priest in 1966 in the Cathedral for the Diocese of Trenton, NJ.

Woodbridge, NJ - First Practices

Fr. Brian McCormick's first assignment was to St. James Parish in Woodbridge, NJ. It was a middle-class town with all the needs of a small city in the late 1960's. He immediately saw opportunities to step in and make his goal of Oneness a reality. In his four years there he inspired a very active CYO (Catholic Youth Organization), began the Bunn's Lane Youth Delinquency House, and organized and ran "Project Understanding", a five-day seminar geared to bringing black and white adults together. It is interesting to note that the issues that he considered important over 50 years ago are still of concern today.

When four years had passed, Fr. Joseph Procaccino, the head of the Trenton Diocesan Office of Clergy, asked Fr. Brian to move to an experimental ministry in Trenton called Martin House. The ministry had been established by the Priests' Council of the Diocese of Trenton to address poverty and racism, while at the same time clarifying the role of the Church in dealing with these issues. The ministry was started in 1968 with three priests volunteering to move to Trenton. By 1970 only one priest was left, and no one else was volunteering. So, the diocese started recruiting. With his experience in Woodbridge, Fr. Brian seemed to be a good choice to keep things going. But Fr. Brian resisted Fr. Procaccino's requests, feeling he was already doing meaningful work in his current parish.

When, after three requests, Fr. Brian prayerfully decided to accept, he did it with a caveat. He said,

> *"If you send me, I'll take it as my first duty to put the Roman Catholic Church of the Trenton diocese on the line as a racist institution. By racist, I don't mean we hate blacks, rather we live at a distance, with fear and hostility that's against the Gospel we hold. And if we hold the Gospel, we have the duty to do something about it."*

And so began his lifelong mission, working for justice for the poor, emphasizing the reality of our society of "Haves and Have

Nots" to the Church and its people, and championing ways to help the underclass.

PART II –
REVELATIONS OF
AN EXPERIMENTAL
MINISTRY

Chapter 2: Martin House

The experimental ministry of the Martin House was conceived and instituted by the Council of Priests of the Diocese of Trenton in 1968. Fr. Brian joined Fr. Bill Dailey there in the Wilbur section in 1970 and stayed for 42 years, much of the time as the only priest in the ministry.

The stated mission of the Martin House, to find ways to address poverty and racism, as well as to determine the Church's role in dealing with this, put Fr. Brian on a firm path. He felt charged with the task of learning about these ills, conveying his findings to the Church and its people, and coming up with ways to deal with the realities he encountered. He recognized more clearly than ever the inter-relatedness of all actions and the Oneness that entailed. He knew he had much to learn about making Oneness a reality just in the Trenton area alone. He set out to live and teach his philosophy that we are all one, and what we do affects everyone else.

When first moving to Trenton, to the dilapidated rowhouse in the Wilbur section where he lived with Fr. Bill, Fr. Brian received mixed messages from his neighbors in the ghetto. He says, "For a while, nothing happened except me getting robbed. I wanted to run away…" But, along with the challenges came good things that helped him bond with the community. One of his first dealings with a neighbor occurred when an energetic boy of about eight came to his door and said, "I'm Jimmy Lee, and I live next door. Do you want to see my dance moves?" Fr. Brian invited him in, as he did many times after that, and became a mentor, with a friendship that endures today. When Jimmy Lee spoke to me about his relationship with Fr. Brian, he said: "Fr. Brian is more than a father to me. He is so responsible for who I am. He taught me how to be a man, an honorable man. He was one of the few adults who would actually listen to kids."

Fr. Brian began to settle in. When the robberies stopped he figured he was probably starting to get accepted. It wasn't until many years later that he learned that another special friend in the neighborhood, Chuck Marini, was responsible for "watching his back" – people were not allowed to "mess with Fr. Brian." However, this did not stop the occasional rock from being thrown through his window – one of which Fr. Brian still displays on his desk.

It was difficult living in the inner city and dealing with his new lifestyle. Fr. Brian often wrote poems or meditations to sort out his thoughts, struggles, and joys. Due to his ever-present difficulty with spelling he relied on a very special person to type and edit these meditations. She was a local woman named Olivia

Dawson, who assisted him with organizing and paperwork and understanding the people of the neighborhood. You can read a poignant poem Fr. Brian wrote about her in Part V.

Olivia was a wonder, but many of the people Fr. Brian dealt with, living in the midst of the poor, were very challenging, giving Fr. Brian reason to think and pray. For instance, there was a time early in Fr. Brian's ministry when he was dealing with a man, Curtis, who repeatedly asked for food, but Fr. Brian found out from the man's son that he had been turning around and selling the food to buy liquor. When Curtis approached him again, coming to his house and insisting, "Hey, Father. I need some food. You're a Father, and you have to help me," Fr. Brian worked through his anger with the following meditation. It is a beautiful example of the situations he faced and the way he thinks and believes.

That little army in me wanted to go to war!
My army sees the truth of the situation.
It would be easier to destroy than to restore.
My army begins to murmur,
"It isn't worth the effort."
Oh, that army is ready to march!

"Wonder-Counselor," my best part is screaming.
"God loves this man - Quickly, how does it fit in?"

Wonder-Counselor says,
"Remember my name is Truth.

All of you must live by the Truth.
"If you do,
He will find: real solutions and achievements.
Your army will always be alive.
The boy will find life and a home.
And God will be found in your midst."

I said, "Curtis, if you don't get out [of my house]
I just might throw you out."
My little interior army of rebels applauds –
I tell'em to shut up.
He leaves.

Alone,
I say to Wonder-Counselor,
"I'm Trusting in You. But it is hard to believe."
But underneath my self-pity,
deep underneath, I wink.
It is really not that hard to believe,
and I have an almost absolute confidence.
Fidelity is the greatest difficulty.
Excerpted from: "What's Happening at the Martin House"
4/6/77 Fr. Brian McCormick

Involve, Rethink, Reorganize – Against a Permanent Underclass

During Fr. Brian's time in the Wilbur section of Trenton, most of the people in the area were African American and not of the

Catholic religion. He respected their beliefs and did not try to actively convert people to Catholicism. He felt Christ wanted him to show the gospel through his life and how he lived it. Still, he wanted the Catholic Church to take a major role in dealing with the urban poor and their problems.

Fr. Brian saw it as his mission and commission to bring his learning and ideas for change to the forefront. After all, the experimental ministry of Martin House had been set up by the Council of Priests of the diocese, and Fr. Brian took his role seriously – frequently writing to the bishop and priests of the diocese telling of what he was learning and doing.

Fr. Brian's own faith and strong attitudes toward what role the Church should play in dealing with the poor were enhanced by living a life with his neighbors in the ghetto. His interpretation of his mission led Fr. Brian to the saying (famous to many of his friends): "Involve, rethink, and reorganize." He knew he had to Involve himself deeply in his ministry, to the point of living in the inner city with the people he served. Then he would Rethink the way things were working. And finally, he would Reorganize a better way to deal with the issues. As he began working with individual issues, he continued to address each one with that approach.

Fr. Brian began organizing Martin House in ways he thought would best minister to the needs of the poor, setting up such activities as Bible studies, summer camp, youth workshops and tutoring. With Lena Meekins of The Mercer Street Friends, Fr. Brian set up workshops on racism that combined black teens from Meekins' After-School Drill Team with suburban CYO groups. Always, the Church's role was paramount in his mind. "I see the main job here as to affect the Roman Catholic Church in this diocese in how it is dealing with the issues of race and poverty: to put the Church on the line."

As Fr. Brian continued to involve himself with the people and to rethink their plight, he formulated into words how the workings of our society create a permanent underclass. Addressing the issues of inequity in our society became the basis of Fr. Brian's life work and can be summed up in an undated commentary he wrote:

> *As a priest and a religious leader, I have looked at our society through the eyes of our compassionate God as He is revealed in the pain of our most neglected brothers and sisters.... It is clear to me that we, as a people, have created a permanent underclass. This permanent underclass is the triplet brother of slavery and the Holocaust. This permanent underclass is created through the dynamics of extortionate profit and usury.*

> *We, as a new generation of men and women of Judeo-Christian values in our American Society, wish in our time to challenge these structures in our society. We see our world moving to armed camps of Haves and Have Nots. We wish to address these issues as we find them in our society.*

This philosophy became the basis of his teachings and his works.

Unstable Housing at the Heart of Poverty

The longer Fr. Brian involved himself with the people, the more he realized that lack of stable housing was a key issue. He was setting up programs and trying to get to know the youth in the area. But he noticed: "We'd have a teenager or youngster in one of our programs for six or eight months and then he'd disappear. I realized that we were dealing not with a stable neighborhood but with a camp of nomads." People moved frequently because they lost jobs (sometimes seasonal) or rents got too high. Fr. Brian could see that frequent moves and the fear of homelessness were at the core of keeping people poor, affecting family life, educational constancy for children, and the pursuit and follow-through of jobs.

Matthew Desmond, author of *Evicted: Poverty and Profit in the American City*, says that millions of people in the U.S. suffer eviction each year, and "the lack of affordable housing sits at the root of a host of social problems, from poverty and homelessness to educational disparities and health care... Eviction is not just a condition of poverty, it is a cause of it."

Without a stable home, people are not able to take advantage of educational and job opportunities. They worry constantly about keeping a roof over their heads. For example, when Fr. Brian helped an enterprising man set up a training program in Trenton for learning the trades, the program's completion rate for students was poor. The men were eager to get the education but missed too many classes due to the instability caused by constantly moving or seeking ways to pay their rent.

It became clear to Fr. Brian that housing for the poor needed to be a top priority for Martin House. But first he needed to examine and understand what the word "poverty" meant to him and to the world at large.

The Definition of Poverty

As Fr. Brian began to "rethink" in his mind the various issues of the poor, he came to see the definition of poverty in his own particular way. He set about to provide housing that was truly affordable to the poor people he was targeting, and he saw that conventional definition of low-income did not fit his group. His people were truly the "sub-poor" – those below 40% median income.

He knew that towns and cities in NJ have requirements to provide a percentage of "low-income" housing, but that it does not often reach the sub-poor, the generational poor. Those he was working with fell into the category of Very Low or Extremely Low Income. The following are HUD Income Levels for a family of four in Mercer County, NJ in 2022. (From *Affordable Housing Hub*)

Median Income
Family of Four in Mercer County, NJ $119.2K
Low Income: $89.4K
Very Low Income: $59.6K
Extremely Low Income: $35.8K

Families categorized as Low Income have a substantially higher median income than those of Very Low or Extremely Low Income. When the requirement for "low-income housing" is defined as having a "Low Income", a variety of residents can be eligible, including educated young people just getting started. This is noble and needed (and, assuredly, much more desirable in the eyes of the municipality), but excludes the generational poor.

You may wonder, why should the sub-poor, those of very low or extremely low income, be helped? Certainly, the families defined as low-income also have a very difficult time. You may even say this is true for the moderate-income people who live on the edge every month and have so many bills. We must consider that the sub-poor have an economic and a mental poverty that is perpetuated from generation to generation. The mindset of poverty needs to be changed in order to break the poverty cycle. These families need an incentive to keep working a minimum wage job, meaning, they need a stable living situation, as well as an upwardly mobile mindset. Yet their lives present so many roadblocks that society tends to consider them as hopeless and leave them behind.

The sub-poor are not served under the existing framework for obtaining low-income housing or even under most homesteading programs. These programs require a strong backing from financial institutions. The system for obtaining low-income housing requires a person to obtain credit from a bank and to make a certain amount of money, and the houses available to them often cost in the $100,000 range.

Even homesteading programs offering abandoned houses to low-income people need to be carefully thought-out. Trenton established a Homesteaders' program around 2015 to provide very low-cost abandoned houses to qualified first-time homebuyers for renovation. But the program required working with a bank for purchase and rehab money. Most of the sub-poor don't have bank accounts or credit cards. After a few community meetings it was realized that the homesteading program was not feasible as it was currently organized.

On April 16, 2016 Joe Tyrrell wrote for NJ Spotlight News:

Trenton 'Homesteading' Program Finds No Takers for Low-Cost Houses

> *Applicants failed to meet financial requirements or weren't ready to rehab a derelict property -- and stay at that address for 10 years. City officials plan another round of public outreach after every applicant in the initial group either dropped out or failed to meet the program's financial requirements. The retooling comes as the Trenton metropolitan area ran up the nation's second-highest foreclosure rate in the first quarter of this year, trailing only Atlantic City. How can the system creatively help those who don't fit in the box? There are so many factors to consider.*

As of mid-2023, there is still no homesteading program available to the poor in Trenton.

Chapter 3: Creating an Unconventional Approach to Housing

Better Community Housing of Trenton

To address the housing situation in Trenton, Fr. Brian established Better Community Housing of Trenton, Inc. (BCHT) in 1972, as an arm of Martin House. The mission of BCHT was to create safe, quality housing in Trenton that very low-income people could truly afford to buy, using their sweat equity to help rehab or build the BCHT houses, while they learned how to care for a home and hopefully picked up some skills of the trades. For these people, going through this process and ending up with their own home would help bring the man and woman together as a family, as well as to create equity, knowledge, self-esteem, and a cohesive community – giving a mindset of hope. All this would be a giant step toward ending generational poverty and fighting a world of Haves and Have Nots.

To make this possible, Fr. Brian had to figure out how to build and finance the houses so that people could actually afford them.

Besides having prospective homeowners put sweat equity into houses both before and after move-in, BCHT would need to build a network of volunteers, as well as tradesmen and suppliers who would discount their time and materials. Financing would come from donations and grants. Additionally, BCHT would hold the mortgages or lease-purchase agreements without interest, so banks would not be involved. Fr. Brian understood that his people would not qualify for a mortgage through a bank, not to mention being able to deal with the gentrification and "redlining" (refusing loans in areas of poor financial risk) that was taking place all over the city.

The discounting of time and materials, donations from generous donors, and the 0% financing held by BCHT differentiated BCHT from other housing programs for the poor. And this allowed Fr. Brian to offer the first houses for only $11,000, well

House sold in 2007 for $21,000

under what it would cost others to build them. The houses built in the 2000's sold for $21,000 and $25,000.

BCHT's program helped provide physical housing and nurture an upward-looking mental mindset for many people. The sweat-equity program required people to work, not only on their own houses, but on others' houses for the duration of their mortgage. This helped give them both the necessary skills to maintain a house and the shared experience of building up a neighborhood and a community.

There are so many people who benefited from BCHT's housing program and who later became instrumental in the workings of BCHT. Very notably there is Pearleen Waters. When Pearleen graduated from Rutgers College in 1982, she got a job working as a probation officer and child support investigator for Mercer County, thinking she wanted to be a lawyer. She was happy with her job, but she could not see how she would be able to pay the high rents being charged in the area. She joined the BCHT homeownership program and eventually moved into a renovated house with her young son and daughter, ages 4 and age 2.

As she continued doing sweat equity and working on the BCHT board, Pearleen got to know the people in her neighborhood and grew her connections in Trenton, which were already very strong because she had grown up there. (If you go anywhere in Trenton with Pearleen, it seems she knows everyone.) Fr. Brian saw the potential in her, and in 1989, asked her to be his administrative assistant at Martin House. He told her that he would pay what she was earning at her current job, but without raises. The draw was that she would be part of the Martin House ministry, helping the people of her neighborhood. Pearleen is a Baptist with a strong faith, and she took on the job as a mission, with determination and dedication, always open to learning more.

Pearleen says, "When Fr. Brian asked me to be his secretary, I had no secretarial skills, but I believed in him. You don't expect white people to come into the community and give something. But he wanted to help the people that no one else cared about, ones who didn't have anything going for them. He saw what needed to be done and used any means possible to get it done. He realized that people needed to be helped in place, where they were. He did that for me and for lots of other people. Fr. Brian also taught me how to learn politics and be community-responsible and how to put into action the things that I had learned from people who had influenced me as I grew up, at the YMCA, the drill team, and at school." Pearleen became an indispensable part of the Martin House team and took seriously the mandate to help people in place, where they were.

Twenty-five years later, when Fr. Brian retired, Pearleen Waters was made the executive director of Better Community Housing of Trenton, and she continues to bring hope to many with her work. She relies on the assistance of other early BCHT homeowners who sit on the Board of Trustees at BCHT. Dorothy Holmes, president, Jacqueline Meyers, secretary, and Tamika Young, community liaison, have been wonderful representatives and advocates for the neighborhood and the Martin House/BCHT projects taking place there, as has Kathy Bellamy, who still lives in her BCHT home across the street from Pearleen.

Another good example of BCHT's success is Jayne Gordon, who in 1989 moved into a renovated BCHT house with her two children. Always an industrious person, Jayne made the most out of owning her own home and eventually sold it and bought something larger to accommodate her many foster children. At Fr. Brian's retirement celebration in 2012, Jayne gratefully wrote:

> *"My life changed when I became a part of the Better Community Housing Program ... which made it possible for a single mom to become a proud homeowner... You and your organization inspired me to become a foster/adoptive parent. ...Better Community Housing of Trenton, Inc. made that dream a reality. You have made a tremendous impact in my life, and I thank you from the bottom of my heart."*

Chapter 4: Relying on the Support of Bishop, Pastors, Lay Volunteers

Fr. Brian knew that for his housing plan to work, he would need strong commitment from the diocese, its parishes, and its people. In keeping with his "We are all One" philosophy, Fr. Brian felt the suburbs in his diocese needed to take responsibility for the cities and that each suburban parish should have a responsible connection to its nearest urban center. He asked the bishop to send letters to pastors telling them about Martin House and asking for support.

This did not happen in the first couple of years, so in 1973 Fr. Brian wrote Bishop George W. Ahr to follow up on a meeting they had. Fr. Brian nudged the bishop, saying,

"We discussed a housing plan... I suggested at this time and in our diocese, we establish as a moral principle: **'The suburbs are responsible to the city.'** You felt in truth this was not so. I am still of the conviction that it is. The difficulty to me seems to be in how it applies. I also suggested that parishes be contacted and their positive active support be sought... I await further discussion with you."

The bishop finally did present the premise of Better Community Housing to the Trenton Diocesan Council of Priests. They, in turn, voted to accept the ministry as part of Martin House and allow Fr. Brian to present it to the pastors of the diocese, which was a positive step. But then there was no follow-up from the bishop asking parishes for their support and participation. After Fr. Brian sent several more pleas to the bishop to get behind the project, the bishop sent out letters to all the parishes in 1977, telling them of the project and asking them to support it.

Fr. Brian had specific, and controversial, ideas on how the suburban parishes should be directly involved with the poor. He sent letters to nearly 200 pastors asking that each church donate $10,000 over three years to be used for a house for the poor, and that each parishioner give one day every two months to work on housing in their nearest urban area. He suggested that each parish establish a ministry which would handle this, possibly forming "supra" parish teams around the diocese where parishes could work together (in Oneness and creating Oneness). He also stressed that those being helped in the urban areas needed to "pay it forward" to others in need.

Bringing pastors and priests to the idea that each parish needs to have a specific program dealing with the poor in the nearest urban center was not an easy task. Many pastors felt that their current parish ministries and duties were difficult enough to accomplish. One priest questioned the concept that the suburbs are responsible to the city, saying that suburbs have their own problems. He suggested that instead of "supra-parish teams" from all over the diocese, as proposed by Fr. Brian, that city priests could form a coalition that would meet once a month as moral support for Fr. McCormick. This, of course, was not at all what Fr. Brian had in mind.

Over the years, Fr. Brian sent many letters to priests in the Diocese of Trenton, trying to impress upon them how important it is for each church to take a responsibility for the poor in its nearest urban center. Fr. Brian's blunt passion for his cause appeared to many priests as critical of their current way of running their parishes.

There is no doubt that Fr. Brian became impatient with the tepid reaction of the bishop and diocesan priests to his message about the poor, but a high school mentor cautioned him to be patient and tried to get Fr. Brian to direct his message in a less confronting manner. Rev. James A. O'Reilly, a former high school coach and mentor, pastor at a Neptune, NJ church in 1978, wrote to Fr. Brian and urged him to be patient and less critical. He wrote, "Your first letter rubbed me the wrong way. Your results showed that I was not the only one who felt that way. Your second letter, Fr. Brian, had a different tenor. That is why, instead of winding up in the waste basket, I read it many times... Speaking as one of our Diocese's "senior priests" and as your old-time mentor, I urge you not to be impatient! ...I ask you not to harshly judge the pastors of your own Diocese... I admire your perseverance and dedication. I honestly would like you to speak to my congregation at all Masses."

Fr. Brian was eventually able to speak about his Martin House/Better Community Housing mission at 14 parishes. He recognized that it was important to bring people from the suburbs into the city to interact, teach, and create with the urban poor, as well as to bring various city groups together to learn from each other. There can be no Oneness without interaction.

While educational, social, and sports programs grew at the Martin House and the community housing program expanded, a dynamic volunteer program emerged. It included parish volunteers as well as students from nearby colleges. The Student Volunteer Council at Princeton University was one of the volunteer groups who worked on renovating houses. A former Princeton student, Sean Zielenbach, recalls that Fr. Brian would get each new group of volunteers together before starting the rehab work and give them "the Gospel according to Fr. Brian." When work time was over, Sean and his friends would sometimes go back to Fr. Brian's kitchen in the old row house, where Fr. Brian would cook them hotdogs. They would talk about Fr. Brian's mission and how he was going about making it work. Sean could see that much depended on how Fr. Brian's strong personality and faith conveyed his convictions and brought people in, but he wondered how what Fr. Brian was doing could be organized into a long-term mission that would endure after Fr. Brian was gone. Thirty-five (35) years later this has, indeed, has become an issue.

Volunteer programs in parishes were key to the success of BCHT. In some parishes, such as Our Lady of Sorrows and St. Gregory the Great in nearby Hamilton, NJ and Our Lady of Lourdes in Whitehouse Station, NJ, parish deacons were instrumental in making the programs work. Parishioners volunteered on Saturdays helping the future homeowners renovate houses. As Fr. Brian watched these people work together, he commented, *"It seems to me that the parable of the Good Samaritan points clearly to who is our neighbor."*

Two men from the nearby parish of Our Lady of Sorrows, Joe Malloy and Jim Brady, began to attend Fr. Brian's 6:30 am Mass each morning at Martin House. After Mass, Fr. Brian and the two men, and anyone else who was interested, would have breakfast in Fr. Brian's kitchen and discuss how they could better "Involve, Rethink, and Reorganize." Many ideas were tossed around and put into action. Jim Brady remembers the vitality and excitement of those breakfast meetings. He recalls that one idea was to start a Christian men's group that could raise awareness of our Oneness and responsibility to each other. In particular, there was Fr. Brian's very idealistic idea to turn the abandoned St. Francis Church in Trenton into a Eucharistic Shrine and a place designed to explore and develop ways for business people and leaders to put Christian ethics into practice in the workplace. In a letter to priests regarding a 1976 meeting with the bishop, Fr. Brian said he had suggested St. Francis become a place:

> "available to the public 24 hours a day... where we would call together politicians, bureaucrats, lobbyists, business, and union people as unique Catholic groups [and talk

about areas] where they felt they were not able to act as Christians [in their work]. I suggested hiring someone like Ralph Nader to do this."

Although the Eucharistic center never got off the ground, in 2018 the Church created a way to bring men together to seek their "spiritual freedom" in the Exodus 90 spiritual exercise for men. Exodus 90 is based on Christ's roadmap for freedom: prayer, asceticism, and fraternity. The spiritual exercise originally started in the seminary but was made available to all men in 2018. It begins with a 90-day guided exercise that can be followed up with ongoing spiritual exercises and participation. As with many things in the Church, we may have to wait a while for this to be offered to women.

Both Jim Brady and Joe Malloy were very involved in renovating houses, and Joe used his architectural skills to design the first multi-family home that BCHT was to build from scratch on Walnut Avenue. Joe kept modifying and perfecting his design as BCHT went on to each new building project, culminating with the construction of ten beautiful homes on Grant Avenue, each having three bedrooms, 1 ½ baths, and a laundry room.

A Role for Deacons

Fr. Brian understood how important deacons could be in organizing volunteers for BCHT and making things happen in their own parishes, and he suggested that a deacon in each parish be given the role of facilitating the parish's work in the nearest urban center.

The deaconate had been reestablished in the Catholic Church in 1966 during Vatican II. The deacon is seen to have the role of enabler and is invited to facilitate the development of the gifts that other members of the Church have. Fr. Brian says that:

> "Theology holds that the deacon is to stand alongside his pastor as part of the sign and symbol of what the Church is. In these mindless superficial times, he is to stand with his pastor as a witness, a sign, and a call that parishioners and parishes need to be involved in the redemptive act of relating to their nearest urban center."

While having parish deacons with a direct connection with BCHT was never formally set into place, there were several deacons who became integral parts of Martin House's Better Community Housing of Trenton.

Deacon Bill Wilson of St. Greg's not only recruited and organized the volunteers, but he used his considerable construction skills to teach both volunteers and prospective homeowners how to do things right while building or rehabbing the houses. He was instrumental in creating the BCHT Job Corps program in connection with Mercer County Vocational Technical School, where the local men could get a high school equivalency diploma (GED) as well as training in the trades, and at the same time, help build houses for BCHT. The program is no longer in existence, but did produce several successful tradesmen. One of its graduates, Jose Rivera, has his own construction business now and credits Fr. Brian for helping him get on the right track for life.

Deacon Joseph Malloy

Another man, Joseph Malloy, who attended Fr. Brian's 6:30 Mass each morning, discerned his calling to be a deacon through his interaction with Fr. Brian at Martin House.

When Joe first told Fr. Brian about his possible calling to the deaconate, he said he wanted to be a deacon at Martin House - which was not a church, per se. But Fr. Brian showed him how important he would be in his own parish in promoting a ministry of volunteers to work with the poor in Trenton, their nearest urban center.

Joe saw the truth in this and was accepted to study to be a deacon for his parish of Our Lady of Sorrows. Joe's ordination as a deacon was celebrated by many people, both from his parish and from Trenton's Wilbur community.

Fr. Brian, in his talk at Joe's ordination as deacon in 1987, said that Joe had deep questions about his own role in a society of Haves and Have Nots. Fr. Brian and Joe discussed this many times. Joe endorsed Fr. Brian's philosophy of extortionate profit and greed (covered more fully in a later chapter) as a basis for poverty and inequity.

Fr. Brian said that Joe functioned as a deacon "enabler" in a very positive way. He saw Joe as a living example of how business people could function morally in our society. "Within the new atmosphere of the physical structure of Our Lady of Sorrows and within the sacramental presence of the Church in the deacon enabler, Joe has found new options that make for less scattering and hurting of people. He is committed as a noble bureaucrat to facilitate the mission he is entrusted with [and helping others see their own potential]."

Fr. Brian felt that "In almost every case, the vitality of the sacramental deacon, letting grace have its way, has provided a way and an opportunity for fellow Christians to live more nobly." Fr. Brian points out examples of fellow Christians who were influenced by Deacon Joe Malloy:

> "There is our friend and Christian brother, Joe Ramus Deputy Director of County Welfare. We feel he has derived a new joy beyond the tired old system of administrative welfare.

> "The deacon enabler encountered his fellow parishioner, Robert Salava. As a builder, he has found a world beyond the ever-expanding acquisition of new business. He has found a way to remember and be responsible to his roots. He has found a way to remember those left behind, those who by the system have been marauded.

> "Eric Cichetti found a new place, a making of a Christian Community. As superintendent of Mercer County Vocational schools, he has found another modest means to help make educational opportunities in vocational training more readily available."

Seeing the great positive influence Deacons Joe Malloy and Bill Wilson had on the people of their parishes, particularly the BCHT volunteers, does make one wonder what could be accomplished if each parish, or cohort of parishes, had a deacon tasked with connecting with the nearest urban center.

Winning Over Tradesmen

As part of Fr. Brian's vision, tradesmen would donate or discount their time and products. He decided to conduct a pilot program where he would recruit tradesmen, talk to them about his ideas, and have them help with the building and rehabbing of houses.

He chose a parish in Highland Park, NJ, then part of the Trenton Diocese, and sent out a request for participants. The tradesmen would meet at the church and address the issue of extortionate profit and usury using Fr. Brian's model of Involve, Rethink, and Reorganize. With the help of the pastor, Fr. Brian identified and sent letters to over 70 tradesmen. Five (5) responded and showed up for his first meeting. This group was able to make some headway in BCHT's housing effort in Trenton, but it was a struggle to maintain this group or form other similar groups. This is an example of how people need reminders of the importance of, and opportunities to share their "wealth."

Builder Frank Kerins

There was one particular tradesman who fell right in with Fr. Brian's ideas and who was a great blessing to Fr. Brian as he imagined and put into practice the workings of BCHT. This special man was an inspiration and a force at BCHT for 15 years, until he died unexpectedly of a heart attack.

Frank Kerins was a construction contractor from Trenton. Frank took time away from his own business to work on the BCHT houses and to teach the trades to teams of homeowners and volunteers. In fact, as an apprentice to Frank, Jimmy Lee Youngblood, Fr. Brian's young dancing friend from next door, who had welcomed Fr. Brian when he first moved to Trenton, grew up to be an electrician. He now has his own business.

Frank told Fr. Brian how important it had been for him to have a role model in the Church in his early working days. His model was Fr. Philip Carey, who was connected with the Xavier Institute of Industrial Relations in New York. In the first half of the 20th century, the Institute had helped organize the labor movement and fought corruption in the unions. Frank and Fr. Brian went to visit an elderly Fr. Carey in the late 1970s and were very impressed with his wisdom and insight, and they sympathized with Fr. Carey's disappointment in the present corruption of the unions. After all, the unions once fought for fair pay for workers as Fr. Brian now fought to get training and decent pay for minorities.

Fr. Carey and Fr. Brian shared similar opinions on how the Church should be involved with enlightening and leading the laity to deal with the poor. It was here that Fr. Brian voiced his question on the role of the Church in conscience formation. Fr. Brian asked: "If priests are the chief formers of conscience in our communities, how many priests understand their role?" Fr. Carey answered, "Not many. And they don't care about the area you are talking about." Fr. Brian asked, "How, then, can the Catholic laity understand its role in the marketplace, what it means to act as an adult Christian?" Fr. Carey just shook his white-haired head and finally admitted that he thought maybe three in 10,000 priests understood. Fr. Brian says that, "After our visit with Fr. Carey, both Frank and I knew what we were up against and sensed what we needed to be committed to." (From Fr. Brian's Eulogy for Frank Kerins)

Building Suppliers

Fr. Brian and Frank Kerins accomplished much, but it wasn't without the help of building suppliers. Two, in particular, became friends and supporters of Fr. Brian, Ernie Ferri (RIP) of Yardville Supply and Kim Coleman of Hamilton Supply. In 1985 Ernie wrote a letter encouraging others in the building industry to become involved in the Martin House ministry, mentioning how he offered goods for cost plus 10% and sometimes lent his trucks and office assistance to Martin House. Kim Coleman of Hamilton Supply remains a supporter of BCHT and Fr. Brian to this day. In 2015, when the BCHT truck broke down, Kim and his brother Keith loaned Fr. Brian a truck for a clothing drive at St. James in Jamesburg. The relationship of the Church to the workplace needs constant nurturing.

Chapter 5: The Realities of Low-Income Housing

"Miracle Houses" Vs. Government-Sponsored Housing

By 1976, BCHT had over 100 volunteers, including about 20 from Joe Malloy's parish of Our Lady of Sorrows. With this team, Fr. Brian had been able to rehab six homes in four years. The homes were sold to very low-income families for $11,000 to $18,000 with payments of a very affordable $100 - $125 a month. The selling price was about half of what the houses cost to build, even at a discount.

The BCHT houses became known as "Miracle Houses." Other low-income housing projects were being built around the city, making use of city, state, and federal funds, but costing much more to build and sell or rent, and also catering to the upper end of the defined "low income" category.

In 1977, Fr. Brian wrote a letter to the newspaper, The Trentonian, about a local low-income-housing project called *"North 25."* He railed against the cost of "low-income" housing and its excessive benefit to banks and builders, the hiring practices that exclude minorities, as well as the lack of responsibility everyone feels (including those who get to live in the new housing) toward "paying it forward" to help others:

Letter to the Editor - Re. North 25 Housing
by Fr. Brian McCormick - Trentonian 11/11/77

"The government is not subsidizing poor folks...In actual fact, the government is subsidizing banks, professionals, and [handlers of building materials] at a very high price [while] sustaining the present power structure... The banks are going to loan this money because it is guaranteed by the government and because... they will make a great deal off of it.... It is clear that these apartments must clear something like $360-$500 a month in rent. That is not giving something to low- and middle- income families. In my mind it is paying extortion money to maintain a style of life at the expense of the material, physical, emotional and spiritual life of others.

"What kind of pressure can we bring to bear that ... this project and similar projects ... (ensure) that minorities are hired and that they be from this city, and, more important, they are truly learning and mastering their trade?

"How can we get over to the one family in 20 that gets into these apartments that now because their lives are more secure they are responsible for affecting the total community, especially those other 19 who can't get decent and financially reasonable housing? A spirit must be generated that says, "Now we will work to make it a little better for others."

Dealing With the City

The path to Oneness is not straight-forward. To achieve his goals in housing, Fr. Brian realized he had to become known to people in the city's administration and learn how to deal with various political elements. He knew he had to use the strength of his personality to convince people of his ideas. He did this and became known among city leaders as "The Father," a force to be reckoned with. When he and BCHT's lawyer showed up at a city council meeting in the late 90's to oppose expanding a junkyard near the local elementary school, people could be heard murmuring, "Uh-oh. The Father is here with the big guns." In the end, the junkyard was removed completely and replaced with a beautiful park with playground equipment and a basketball court.

At one point, Fr. Brian spoke to the city of Trenton about adopting his model for low-income housing, saying it would be much more economical and would have a positive societal impact, lessening the gap between the Haves and Have Nots.

Although Fr. Brian's plan was not adopted by the city, the city did help BCHT to acquire property at minimal cost and identify government funding sources.

In truth, Fr. Brian's plan for providing truly affordable housing to the poor was complex in nature. It did not follow conventional models for 'affordable housing', but, as noted earlier, it worked at getting suppliers and tradesmen to donate or discount their goods and time. It required future inner-city homeowners to work on their own homes, and it required volunteers from the suburbs to work alongside them. As far as financing went, Fr. Brian felt it was necessary for BCHT to seek donations and grants and to be the loan provider for the homebuyers rather than a financial institution.

The East State Street Housing Project

Dealing with the bureaucracy, strictures, and politics related to city, state, and federal rules for low-income housing was challenging, and Fr. Brian has many stories to tell about this. One of the more frustrating and interesting examples can be found in a later BCHT project, the East State Street Project. The original plan for 30 townhouses was designed at a discounted rate by renowned architect Michael Graves from nearby Princeton, NJ. As a footnote: Princeton is 10 miles away from Trenton in distance and millions of miles away in the makeup and structure of its city. Princeton gains financial support from Princeton University, has excellent schools, a largely well-to-do and educated populace, and it is a very desirable and expensive place to live.

Mr. Graves provided BCHT with a plan for 30 townhouses in small clusters with convenient parking plazas, all to be built on abandoned property owned by the city of Trenton.

In 2002, the city offered BCHT land on East State Street, indicating there was $5.4 million in funds available for demolition and housing from the Balanced Housing Grant/Loan Program. BCHT would provide $600,000-$700,000 from its "100 Homes for 100 Families" campaign. The transaction dragged on, and the property sat in limbo. By 2005, the city no longer had money to demolish the abandoned houses on the property. The county then offered BCHT $260,000 for demolition, not pointing out that the funding had certain restrictions requiring all units to be handicap accessible (adding new design and building requirements and costs to the budget). This was burdensome at the time, but became a blessing for elderly, sick, or injured homeowners.

In the meantime, new environmental laws went into effect, and it was discovered that a large part of the land was too polluted, by current standards, to have houses built on it. Much of the soil and fill on the property would have to be excavated and removed, leaving land that required EPA monitoring for many years to come.

In 2006, the Balanced Housing funding was lowered from $5.4 million to $3.5 million, and the city insisted that BCHT still take over the entire property, even though they could only build on a portion of it. The new design for 20, rather than 30, townhouses meant reconfiguring the housing clusters into larger groups, which created the need for a homeowners' association (not an easy thing to handle in a low-income project). In addition, there would be a large grass-covered area that could not be built on but needed to be maintained and monitored for pollution.

To shorten a long story, the architectural and engineering companies resigned and had to be replaced. Finally, in 2009, a new design was approved, led by architect Russell DiNardo. Clearances and permits were obtained, and work began on the 20 new townhouses.

It was not until 2012 that the first homeowners moved in, 10 years after the initial plans had been made. There were fewer houses than originally planned, and the cost to build the 20 units and the park across the street was $4.3 million, supported by a $3.5 million grant from the Balanced Housing Grant/Loan Program, $260,000 from Mercer County for demolition, and $85,000 from Regional Contribution Agreement funds.

Fr. Brian on E. State St.

The remaining amount was provided by donations to Better Community Housing of Trenton. With the completion of the East State Street project in 2012, the total number of homes built or rehabbed by BCHT reached 167.

Although the average cost for building the 20 East State Street homes (not to mention the pollution remediation and building of the park) was much more than originally specified, BCHT kept its promise to keep the homes truly affordable to very low-income families by selling each unit for only $25,000, with a monthly payment of about $225, plus property taxes and utilities. As with all its homes, **BCHT was again able to do what other organizations could not – provide houses to families under 40% median income that they could actually afford to buy.**

After all the trials and setbacks, the East State Street Project culminated in a positive way with the receipt of a 2015 Phoenix Award to the City of Trenton and its building partners for the 20 homes and the new Greg Grant Park across the street. The award recognizes exemplary brownfield redevelopment and revitalization. The homes and park are located on three former industrial sites that were contaminated with toxic products.

Chapter 6: The Root of Poverty – Fr. Brian's Philosophy

The Truth About the Poor

I think a prophet can be defined as someone who tells you what you would rather not hear... If I'm right about that, then Fr. Brian McCormick may qualify as a prophet. He doesn't believe that ... the needs [of the poor] in the country at large can be met within the present order of things. [He says] there are poor people in our cities because the rest of us are greedy. Brian calls one institutional aspect of this greed by a technical name: "extortionate profit and usury." *By Charles Paolino*

The News Tribune, July 14, 1992 Woodbridge, NJ

Society's Greed – Extortionate Profit and Usury

Fr. Brian was, and still is, convinced that the structure of our whole society is based on greed, which leads to "extortionate profit and usury." He cites, in particular, the building industry – in the awarding of contracts, unreasonably high budgets, accepted change orders and cost overages due to specific requirements that benefit certain suppliers or tradesmen, etc..

Fr. Brian came to clearly see the effect of greed as he put into practice his adage, Involve, Rethink, and Reorganize:

(Involve) As Fr. Brian got to know the people of the Wilbur section of Trenton and started ministering to their needs, he began to see that poverty stemmed from the basic greed of human beings, leading to a society that is organized to make the rich richer and the poor poorer [Haves and Have Nots].

(Rethink) Fr. Brian became convinced that the Church needed to be a strong moral leader in the formation of conscience for the people. The problems of the poor, particularly in education and housing, needed to be recognized and addressed by parishes, which would lead their people.

(Reorganize) Fr. Brian did not just state his beliefs. He took action to convey them to others and to make them happen. As previously noted, he wrote to the bishop and all the pastors in the diocese, pointing out his conclusion about systemic societal greed.

As pointed out by the therapist while he was at the seminary, Fr. Brian looked at the whole picture and then figured out how all the pieces were interrelated. (Then he would re-organize things.) In this way he looked at poverty and many of society's ills as stemming from the basic human instinct of greed – in the way we conduct business, deal with others, and think mainly about ourselves. He feels these ills are systemic to our society and are due to lack of recognition of the Oneness or the inter-relatedness of our society.

One Man's Take on Greed

Fr. Brian likes to use Deacon Joe Malloy as an example of how business people should think about their part in creating One-ness. He pointed this out in his sermon for Joe's ordination as a deacon in 1987:

> "Joe asked, 'Do I have a right to have a job for the state and do little? I feel I participate in a system of welfare by attendance.'

> "[In examining this] we sensed together that, if one knows the structure one is serving is not fulfilling its public mission and [if one] is benefiting from it while the structure hurts others, we need to tax ourselves in time, money and effort to help those abused. We cannot simply blame others and the structure [society] and go along with the agenda.

> "As life and opportunity would have it, Joe was able to leave that employment and, with a Christian friend and partner, began [his own architectural firm, which] had to interface with the secular world [in an] age in need of creative adaptations."

In the same sermon, Fr. Brian went on to explain what kind of creative adaptations might be made in our world:

> "This entrenched tired world tries to tell us we cannot undertake being just to, and responsible for, the world. Except...it is not true. The Christian heart and mind are touched and powered by the very presence of the living God and the loving Jesus.

> "All need to learn to be responsibly free! All need to learn to be responsibly caring. Then together in gratitude and worship, in love and joy, we can build to live together for billions and billions, and possibly for the expanding cosmos."

Fr. Brian said that Joe Malloy understood that "the self-centered pursuit of individual remuneration in the system he served left out many people... Legally, no one is held liable. Morally, we see it clearly as thievery and marauding." He noted that Joe had challenged: "Do I have a right to charge 18% to 22% as an architect-builder?"

After much discussion the bottom-line answer was, "No". Joe asked, "Then I should charge less?" After more discussion the answer they arrived at was "No. If you charge less, it just goes back into the same pockets that are keeping it all for themselves."

Fr. Brian responded to Joe with his idea for dealing with "extortionate profit." He said:

"You need to charge the going rate, then tax yourself in some creative manner. Tax yourself in your time, involvement, money. A concept to think about would be a 20%-30% self-tax, which is specific in three areas, a) relate in the nearest urban center, b) relate in the third world, and c) creation of a Christian upper business morality group."

Fr. Brian was able to put forth many of his ideas on greed and recognizing the "Oneness" of humanity in his sermon for Joe's ordination. He concluded by asking whether it was possible to create a new order that included:

"Black and white able to create a new synthesis of high values and a personal lifestyle that lets us come together as equal brothers and sisters... Can God do it? Joe and I believe He can." Fr. Brian asks, "Will you join us?"

"Wealth that does not dominate or unduly motivate. A new start by a new birth of youthful, informed Christians will seek to create a new world and joyfully and confidently put up with their share of the sufferings of Christ... Can God do it? Joe and I believe He can." Again, Fr. Brian asks, "Will you join us?"

Adult Morality

In 1976, Fr. Brian wrote a letter to his bishop regarding "adult morality". He felt that everyone, within the leadership of the Church, must recognize and deal with the real moral problems of people living in the world. His ideas might be considered naïve, or perhaps just filled with faith (through God all things as possible). Fr. Brian said that so many problems stem from high rates: "No bankers [should] live comfortably with today's interest rates. A forum is needed to find out how we can bring capital under human control.

He went on to say that "the heart of this is to develop the model that people pursue a career (a vocation) that leads to the development of essential goods, as opposed to superficial goods, the idea of essential goods developed within the understanding of the needs of the world community."

Specifically, Fr. Brian is concerned with:

- "[What is] the [reasonable] percent of profit that can legitimately be made on one's effort [or how that profit can be shared for the good of others.]
- "The idea that all must work – work seen as the purposeful organization of one's human energies to a clearly perceived worthwhile goal and the pursuing of that goal with effectiveness and efficiency.
- "The idea that everyone has the responsibility to make their community better by concrete action and involvement."

Our Society Creates a Permanent Underclass

"In fact we often consider only the superficial and instrumental causes of poverty without attending to those

harbored within the human heart, like greed and narrow vision." Pope Benedict XVI, 2009 World Day of Peace

As noted earlier, Fr. Brian feels a culture of Haves and Have Nots is endemic to our society. In an article called *The Secret Infidel* published in "The Last Word" column of the June 15, 2012 edition of *Commonweal* (a Catholic Review of Religion, Politics & Culture), Fr. Brian speaks about how a permanent underclass is created by our society.

> "Our political and economic system concentrates power and wealth in the hands of a small minority and so guarantees the existence of a permanent underclass, whose members live without stable employment, decent housing and proper education and health care."

In the same *Commonweal* article, Fr. Brian reminds us that government and NGO programs for the poor do not take away personal accountability.

> "Programs administered by governments and NGOs purport to address the problems of poverty. An affluent Christian may think these programs free him from any personal responsibility for the poor. This is an illusion. As Pope Benedict XVI has written, 'What the fight against poverty really needs are men and women who live in a profoundly fraternal way and are able to accompany individuals, families, and communities on journeys of authentic human development.'" (*The Secret Infidel*)

The human tendency to revere the status-quo (Haves and Have Nots) and keep it maintained informs our society's actions. In the article, Fr. Brian points out that Pope Francis declared on his 10th anniversary as Pope:

> *"It is increasingly intolerable that financial markets are shaping the destiny of people rather than serving their needs, or that the few derive immense wealth from financial speculation while the many are deeply burdened by the consequences."*

In combatting the status quo of Haves and Have Nots, Fr. Brian quotes Zacchaeus (Luke: 19, 6-9) as a model.

> "The Church has a pastoral obligation to challenge the human tendency to consider maintenance of the status quo our most important goal. Here Zacchaeus ought to be our model. He rejected the notion that he was entitled to profit at other people's expense. He realized that personal conversion involved a commitment to justice. Scripture tells us that he would give half of what he had to the poor and make restitution 'fourfold' to those he had wronged as a tax collector." (*The Secret Infidel*)

According to *The Secret Infidel*, Fr. Brian feels that the crisis twenty-first century America most needs to address is "not secular persecution or forced conversion to Islam, but the 'secret infidel' that lives within every Christian, the nonbeliever willing to go through the motions of a ritual but unwilling to risk his own comfort."

He goes on to say: "The separation of daily life from the word of God can be quantified in the form of unreasonable profits and excessive interest. Our economic system not only fails to act in the interest of the truly poor but often acts against their interests," such as the gentrification of urban areas where the poor are pushed out.

Pope Benedict XVI reinforced the premise that no one should benefit economically at the detriment of others. In his Encyclical Letter *Caritas in Veritate*, 2009, he said:

"The dignity of the individual and the demands of justice require that economic choices do not cause disparities in wealth to increase in an excessive and morally unacceptable manner...through the systemic increase of social inequality... Social cohesion suffer[s], thereby placing democracy at risk."

A Creed to a National God of Power

At Christmas 1994, Fr. Brian sent out a poem he had written that spoke of what he feels our country takes as its creed. Harking back to the Nicene Creed, it is cynical but disturbingly true.

> We believe in our Country, right or wrong
> for it is the greatest and most powerful
> decider of what is worthwhile for all.

> We believe in Power,
> our most noble offspring,

first begotten and most honored,
the exact image of its generator.
A necessary offspring.

It is through it
that all other images take on form.
For us men and for all our good
it regulates all of our lives

By its twin – law,
Power took on flesh and became us.
For our sake it crucified the non-conformer.
It legislated, enforced and killed.

Immediately there was order in the land
In fulfillment of its decrees.
Power enthroned itself on high
and rules as a flag over the land.

It will come again, and again, and again
to judge those living on its land.
For it fears its kingdom will end.

We believe in its twin – law,
that it tells us what is worthwhile,
that follows all the prompting of Country and Power.

With Country and Power
it is worshipped and glorified.

It has spoken through the Courts.

We believe hysterically
that all this will keep together.
We look to be the greatest, right now,
and to obtain the good life, right here.

Let it be so!

INTERLUDE

Let Us Be One - Suburb and City

Before following further on Fr. Brian's life journey, let us pause to think upon one of his meditations that calls for Oneness in suburb and city, while showing us the type of person who is left out when society (people and clergy) care more for their own comfortable way of living than for what they can do to make the world a better place. Fr. Brian defines this meditation as "a search for certitude in faith, a confirming of responsibility." He gives the man in the meditation the name Peniel because, as in Genesis, this man represents the face of God. (From the 1977 meditation: Faith/Responsibility – See Part V for remainder)

Around 10:10 –
I hear a knock on my window, a rap on my door.
In bounds my friend Peniel (Gen 32:30).
My second door flies open. The bottom pane shatters!

"Don't tell me!"
this Quasimodo figure screams at me.
Down his dark, black face blood streams.

He is hunched over, screaming,
a knife waving in his right hand.

He says, "Look - look at my face.
Look - look at my arm. Look - look at my finger.
"You say, 'Turn the other cheek.'
and they hit you in the face with a brick.
"You say, 'Be nice, get along.'
and they cut you with a knife."
"Well, no more for me,
I'm going to kill me a nigger ~ No, Fr. Brian!"

Now he is in my kitchen;
"No!" - he screams. I'll kill me one of 'em."
And again and again and again he stabs my luan kitchen door.
Not once, but nine times. He punches a hole in it.
He smashes a chair against the table,
puts his fist through our hockey game,
throws my drawer across the floor,
seeking other knives.

I keep talking to him.
After thirty-five to forty minutes
his family has gathered
and he rushes out to continue the mayhem!

This is not a relating of mayhem.
It is a search for certitude in Faith;
a confirming of responsibility.

Later that night I reflect on those events!
I am sure, Lord, **that man**
is the creation of our unbelieving irresponsible society.

Now imagination is running wild.
I fantasize the circus - yes, I see the lion tamer.
At the end of the show he snaps his whip.
The lion... Paws.
The lion... Howls.
The lion... Fretfully backs into his cage.
Down slide the bars.

How, in my imagination
I desire to produce this fantasy...

As Peniel comes into my house (32:31 Genesis)
I quickly get one of my assistants
to back my truck up to my door.
On the truck is a cage.

As Peniel runs around stabbing doors,
breaking furniture,
Saying, "Never turn the other cheek. KILL. "
I grab my whip.
I back Peniel in to the awaiting cage.
As he fretfully retreats,
we drop the cage door over him.

Our witness of great urgency – captured!
Now ~ to bring him into a situation that calls for...
Faith:
  Jesus wants to redeem him,
    and the world that does this to him
Responsibility:
  A clear knowledge, that is,
    (how should faith come if no one speaks?)
  A clear knowledge, that is,
    (we must deal with this)
  A clear knowledge, that is,
    (we have but two choices:)
      1. crucify this madman out of our existence
          and justify ourselves, or
      2. respond to his pain by anointing him
          with the spirit of compassion that pledges itself to bear
          the maddening pain that has caused this insanity

In my imagination
in fear (knowing the danger that is Christianity), and
in joy (knowing that together in faith and responsibility
with this man we can find the path that can redeem us all.)
For I am convinced I can't be saved, unless,
I am not only for, but with, the least of my brothers.

I will race to the "poor in spirit"
as the suburbs so like to call themselves.
My truck comes to a halt!
I back up to the rectory door.

I leap from my truck.
The thud of my feet echoes all the way up my back
putting goose bumps on my head.

I leap the porch of the suburban rectory.
My finger presses the illuminated button.
Seconds, like years, pass.
The rectory door swings open. The redeeming Father stands.

l open the cage door of my truck.
Out leaps our man in need of our redemptive love!

What shall we do together, fellow priest?

The last line points out a key question in Father Brian's philosophy - and should be food for thought for all of us.

PART III –
CO-CREATING WITH GOD – OUR WORLD AND OUR ETERNITY

Chapter 7: Co-Creation

Most all of us wonder about the after-life – heaven, hell, eternity, perhaps purgatory, or even nothingness. Fr. Brian believes that heaven and hell are simply convenient constructs, created to explain in simple terms what happens when we die. Rather than an after-life of heaven and hell, Fr. Brian believes we are constantly co-creating, with God, the world around us and who we will be in the hereafter, that God reveals this to us in the after-life, when we die. This is a life-altering idea and a huge responsibility.

Fr. Brian says that what each individual does in a lifetime creates the society we live in, that "you are the world." This life of co-creation determines who we will be and how we will relate to God for all eternity. He feels that God does not judge us when we die, He simply reveals to us who we are. The possibilities are endless.

An Epistle to Successful Christians

In a letter to a friend with questions about his existence, Fr. Brian wrote:

We live a life of certain death and the promise of everlasting 'being-who-we-have-created.' Existence is the given gift. What we do from the base of existence co-creates forever what we will be.

Love is the issue. God is love. All of life moves under the organized hand of humanity. We build structures. We mediate our responsible love relationship through the structures we create and make viable.

The truth that is at stake in our society for a successful Christian business person is that 'we are doing well only if all are doing all right.' To love one's neighbor as oneself is the simple demand of our God-given gifted nature.

If humanly organized world structures disproportionately favor certain groups to the absolute disadvantage of others, then the everlasting Christian must seek to address those structures to at least the direct proportion that one benefits from and cooperates in those structures...

The above principle seems to be made present to us who are the children of moms and dads who brought us through to a materialistically better life [than theirs]. It seems to me that their life, and our everlasting dignity, demands of us that we address these issues in our culture.

Friend, that would be my Epistle. I would hope we could think this through together, and for the good of people, find ways of applying it. (By Fr. Brian McCormick 9/5/89)

Confronting Greed

Fr. Brian proposes that greed debilitates the spirit, that is, we let it become the master in our society. In an opinion article in a March 2017 BCHT newsletter, he said:

As a culture we have a very grave problem: we create a culture of materialism that debilitates the demands of the spirit.

In Christian terms it is said in Matthew that, "No man can serve two masters. He will be attentive to one and despise the other. You cannot give yourself to God and money. I warn you, then do not worry about your livelihood, what you are to eat or drink or use for clothing. Is not life more than food? Is not the body more valuable than clothes?"

"You cannot serve two masters." This is confronting. Does this mean we have no choice – meaning, we will serve one or the other? As a brother with all Christians, I am sure that is exactly what it means.

Consider "attentive to one and despise the other." A better expression for "despise" might be apathetic toward. Ask, what holds our attention, what are we interested in, what excites us in our communication, readings and reflective thinking? And what do we "despise"?

Jesus breaks down his thought to my level. He redefines "master" as money. He redefines "money" as livelihood, eating and drinking and being clothed. Does our attention ever get beyond these? Is it possible that we despise or are apathetic to anything that doesn't somehow hook into our preoccupation with livelihood?

People may be concerned with qualifying with the right credentials to the arbitrary standards of upward mobility, or with interest rates and investment plans. Rather, shouldn't we be working to build a community that will give us the security we need in later life, using our ability to direct the free gift of the world and its resources so that all our brothers and sisters can live well?

We openly, or possibly secretly, want a splendid temporal livelihood – so much so, we are jealous of those who have it. And so, our spirits are also debilitated.

What would it mean to create social structures that do not worship money and possessions? In our culture we are trained to distance ourselves from the poor, to give in a unified way from our abundance and thereby create the illusion and the image that we are effective and successful with the poor. I believe that even our contributions at our worship services are a mutual buy-off between clergy and congregation, so that we never have to ask anything significant of each other, to get to the in-depth places of spirit and truth. ["Buy-off" is very harsh, but this is so typical of Fr. Brian's epistemology.]

If only we would face the overwhelming pressure in our society to be concerned exclusively with the acquisition of material possessions, we could see the new spiritual power an attentive person must bring to his society. The redemptive message of Jesus that is needed in our society was captured by Pope John Paul II. He said in Yankee

Stadium that we are called upon "to give to the poor not from our abundance but from our subsistence."

Because our culture and the ease by which, through pleasure and business, we go along with and conform to the structures of our society, I believe we despise to the point of intolerance and apathy the deeper truths that Jesus calls us to. He has indeed said, "Your heavenly Father knows all that you need. Seek first his kingship over you, his way of holiness, and all these things will be given you besides." Matt. 6, 24-25:33

The Twin Towers

By 1994, Martin House and Better Community Housing of Trenton had expanded greatly. With the monetary help and physical work of many, they had built two buildings, one each on the northwest and southwest corners of East State Street and Chambers Street. The building on the right housed the priests, a used clothing store, and rooms for conducting BCHT business, programs, and community meetings. On the left was the 8,000 square-foot Martin House Learning Center for the education of neighborhood children and adults.

Fr. Brian deemed the buildings "The Twin Towers." To him these buildings stood for Martin House's position against worldly greed and ostentation, represented so clearly at the time by the Twin Towers of New York's World Trade Center.

He saw the buildings as a powerful symbol of the presence of God in Trenton, reminding the world of the work being done to co-create, with God, a just world, in contrast to Manhattan's Twin Towers, which represented the epitome of wealth, greed and status.

Chapter 8: Systemic Issues Require Church as Leader

If Fr. Brian is correct, greed and selfishness are systemic to our society. So, how do we address this issue? What is really needed is to recognize the fact that "it takes a village" to address the issue of poverty. There needs to be recognition of the problem (by a majority of society) - as well as a sincere desire to make a difference, along the lines of Fr. Brian's call to bring everyone to the understanding that we are all one – "you are the world." What any one person does affects the whole, including how we distribute profits.

Fr. Brian would say that fighting poverty requires private sponsorship and financing rather than relying on financial institutions. Corporations and wealthy people need to have an integral part in fighting poverty, with their money behind them, as well as a passion for righting the ills of society. At the same time, those in need must learn to take charge of their lives and work to make things better for themselves. As Fr. Brian likes to say, "Life is no magic show where you just pop into heaven."

This raises the question – how does this position of Oneness become known and integral to the mind of the people?

The Role of Pastors and Parishes – "Keepers of Conscience"

We must "comfort the afflicted and afflict the comfortable." Chaplet of Dorothy Day and Peter Maurin

Fr. Brian exhorts us to address the issue of systemic greed and inequality (lack of love of neighbor) by co-creating and making changes that produce a more just society. This seems an insurmountable task. Fr. Brian feels that it is here that the Church is called upon to be a special arbiter and informer. The Church must help define the issues and take responsibility to convey them to the people. Few other institutions could have such a powerful voice around the world.

Fr. Brian feels that the role of the Church must be to inform peoples' consciences in such a way that enables a just society to exist. In an essay, *Christian Keepers of Conscience,* Fr. Brian agrees with Dorothy Day's message above, and says:

> *"If, instead of flattering their flock's moral vanity, our priests and bishops would challenge them to repudiate greed, more middle-class Catholics might take personal*

responsibility for the authentic human development of their brothers and sisters in need."

In the same essay, Fr. Brian is insistent that the Church needs to inform the conscience of a people for whom the culture conditions them to accept luxury as rightful.

> *"The parish is a place to arouse consciences, inspire conversion, prompt action. The parish is not a sanctuary designed to offer uncritical self-assurance – 'God, I thank you that I am not like other men.' Too many people turn from the comforts of the liturgy back to the pursuit of their own comfort and security without regard to how their pursuit affects others. They are conditioned by a culture that regards luxury as the measure of a successful life."*

Fr. Brian wrote a letter to the bishop of Trenton, saying that the Church had "fallen out of contact with the real dynamics of this world and how it has to be organized."

> *"There has been a loss of the vision of social justice, and the vigor to pursue a difficult course. There are priorities in this day and age, that a parish, as a corporate body of many members in Christ, needs to pursue a concrete program relating to its most proximate pocket of poverty."*

Fr. Brian took the leadership role of the Church so seriously that he brought together a group of deacons and other involved volunteers in 1972 to help him formulate an extensive formal proposal on how the Church should be involved in issues of race and inequality. Thanks to supporters like Norman Diegnan, Chuck Paolino, and others he was able to present a well-thought-out and comprehensive proposal for how the parishes in the diocese could become "involved in meeting the racial tension of our society and servicing all God's people." The proposal gave a detailed course of action, broken into five basic steps.

1. Establish Parish Responsibility (obtaining money for staff and a place for a central agency)
2. Create Sermons for All Parishes for Lent 1973 that address racial issues and call for leaders and actions to address the issues
3. Survey of Priests by college youth regarding awareness and attitudes toward racial issues and racism
4. Educational Training Course for a group of interested people at each parish (social action committee), based on the book, *Crisis in Black and White*
5. Community Awareness Program by the social action committee – 8-Week Lecture/Film Series brought by the parish to the (racially mixed) community

The full proposal was very detailed and specific, but no part of it was pursued. Fr. Brian felt that the lack of engagement was well-stated in a comment from *The New Evangelization for the*

Transmission of the Christian Faith by the Synod of Bishops XIII Ordinary General Assembly:

> *"Perhaps… the problem of unfruitfulness in evangelization and catechesis today can be seen as an ecclesiological problem which concerns the Church's capacity, more or less, of becoming a real community, a true fraternity and a living body, and not a mechanical thing or enterprise."*

Could now be the time to put an educational program like this into action?

The Priest's Role

To define the role that priests should play in conscience formation, Fr. Brian decided to first examine priests' reactions to his philosophy. In 1984 he interviewed 22 pastors about their reactions to his ideas about how parishes should get involved with the poor, as well as what he considered the four major concerns of the laity. He released his findings in a letter to priests and the bishop in 1984. The letter did not garner much reaction.

In 2020, Fr. Brian revisited his 1984 findings in a letter to priests of the diocese (1984-2020PriestsSumLtr.docx). Fr. Brian reminded priests of what he had concluded in 1984, saying that very little had changed in his eyes, and that the findings were still timely. What Fr. Brian wrote to priests is lengthy but worth reading and contemplating:

"I sense from priests that the Spirit has placed a model of parish in our hearts: the people of God, as a whole, must truly trust in God, be of service to all their brothers and sisters, and remain in a state of journey.

"Where I think we are failing badly is that we respond both to God's inspiration and our neighbors' needs from a superficial emotional response... We are loving the Lord our God with our whole heart, but we have completely forgotten about our whole mind.

"I believe the following is co-natural to the conditions of our world and parish, and what the redeeming Lord of History wishes us to do today.

- "An affluent society, preoccupied with self, must be challenged and trained not to look at the 10% above them but rather at the 90% below them. In a society that needs gratitude toward the past instead of the assumption of personal privilege for the present, we must organize effectively to demonstrate that the concerns of the Gospel are the true priorities of the New Body of Christ — The Parish.
- "I suggest a very simple approach to acquiring sobriety in a very intemperate world. Every parish ought to tax itself 10% of its ordinary income. This does not include what ought and needs to be sent to the office of the bishop.
- "When we tax ourselves this 10%, it ought to be broken up into three parts: 1/3 to the nearest urban center, 1/3 to the most proximate pocket of poverty, 1/3 to a third world country."

This startling and challenging declaration was followed by further insights on how the Church should guide the people to make all this happen. In the same letter, Fr. Brian wrote:

"The new model of the Church which the Spirit seems to be leading us to, demands we live with and commit ourselves to trust in God, serve all of our brothers and sisters, and remain in a state of lifetime journey. This 'ecclesia' calls us to organize the people of God, founded around the Eucharist, in the local Christian Community.

"In order to complement the impetus of the Spirit, there is the necessity of a process. In today's world, no one should be seen as responding to the Gospel unless they are undertaking a process of Involve, Rethink, and Reorganize. We, as followers of Jesus, seek with His courage to discover the real evils and, with redemptive love, challenge them unto death. This is the true meaning of the cross – not some relic of wood but the continuous mystery of the redeeming God in our personal history.

"I also see that we must keep in mind three realities:

- "The Little Picture - We must do what we are doing with attention, excellence, and non-violence.

- "The Big Picture – However, using our mind, we must see with exactness how this little picture fits into the Big Picture of local, national, and international life.

- "The Kingdom of God – Lastly, both the Little Picture and the Big Picture must be viewed constantly in reflective prayer under the light of the Kingdom of God."

"I would ask you to think seriously about the Big Picture. If in truth we would let ourselves be informed about the Big Picture of how things are accomplished in this free and dynamic world, and if we saw how others suffer because of the benefits we receive in our consuming lifestyle, then a different sense of urgency would touch our lives. If we are truly to love God with our whole mind, we must examine how we conduct both our private and corporate lives. Our conduct will ultimately fall under the true final judgment of God. Honestly, I sense an excitement and urgency which I wish as a gift to all."

In the same summary letter, Fr. Brian said he felt that, "The general reactions to these concerns, by the 22 pastors I spoke to [in 1984], was basically monotone. One priest said that he thought the problems were there but he didn't think these were as absolute or as pervasive as I was making them. In general, there was an agreement that these problems exist. It usually stopped there. Then there was a move [by pastors I was interviewing] into talking about what this particular parish was doing."

Meeting the Concerns of the Laity

Fr. Brian knew that, for the Church to reach the people, it had to understand their needs and thought processes. He was able to hear, and, in a small way, to understand the minds of people who volunteered and built houses and designed programs with him at Martin House. He felt there were several issues that should be of concern to priests, and he stated these in the above mentioned 1984/2020 letter to priests. He felt that some key concerns of the people were related to their lack of understanding of the theory of co-creation:

NOTHING MATTERS: There is no pastoral concept of God's true final judgment. From our Churches, the impression is being given that God's mercy will cover all we have done or failed to do, that all we have to do is believe, and no matter what we do, if there is a heaven, we will get in.

AGNOSTICS: The age group of Catholics between 40-50, who have been moderately successful in business in an uncritical manner, are becoming agnostics.

CONFUSED: The age group of Catholics between 40-50, who planned (or limited) their families to two children, are now finding themselves in an empty house. They have no real purpose.

HURT AND DISAPPOINTED: The age group of 30-40, who have high ideals, are now finding themselves compromised. They are discovering that the very way they are making a living causes the problems they wish they could help. They are quietly hurting with hostility and fear. They are rejecting the Church because it has given no effective leadership, direction, or support.

In a 1976 Commentary and Sharing sent to the bishop, Fr. Brian talked about what priests might do to address the needs of the people and build a society of justice. He felt many priests did not recognize what they had to offer. He said priests must:

" Fully understand what they can give to the world:

> "It seems to me we [priests] are hesitant leaders who at best are holding together the little we have. I believe both our Father and the times demand of the good householder a vision which is wider and a leadership that is much more vibrant. We surely lack something. I believe it is that we, as priests, don't truly understand how much we have to give to the world. It is my opinion we must begin to think of a whole new society built on Christianity and delivering justice."

"Preach more about Jesus as a role model for human existence, to imitate Jesus' life as we are incorporated into the Church:

> "More and more I am convinced that the greatest problem faced today [among the laity] is the search for any meaning in life. If my judgment

is right, it seems to me we need to preach much more, and much more openly, about Jesus. We must from this perspective think much more about what incorporation into the Church truly means."

To make a point about recognizing who Jesus is to us, Fr. Brian wrote a meditation in about 1999, in a Christmas letter (New Glories Entrusted to Us – See Part V). It was directed to all who "wake in the morning with that feeling that nothing, absolutely nothing, really means anything." He encourages these people to recognize that Jesus is the answer to life. They must see the "new glories that God has entrusted to us" – to follow a new star (make a change), hear a new song and respond to it. In this meditation, he says:

> *If we truly believe not only in God*
> *but in His birth into our evils,*
>
> *His birth is our birth*
> *into the vocation of being God's power*
> *to bear the burden*
> *to redirect our destructive direction.*

In the same meditation, Fr. Brian goes on to explain Jesus' "birth into our evils" this way:

> *Christmas is no pretty, pleasant story.*
> *It is the event by which our Father gave to the world*
> *the bravest man to be in creation to show us how to live.*

The Rigors of Being a Priest

Besides the challenge of determining how to organize a parish and interact with the laity, a priest must face the solitude of his lifestyle. At Christmas 1990, Fr. Brian shared his feelings in a letter to priests. He said that Christmases spent alone should not be sad, but rather, they should be an opportunity to truly sense the presence of God:

> *This is not God's grace-filled moment*
> *for his most dedicated ones.*
>
> *This moment, heard rightly, is an invitation*
> *To be peaceful, to consider, to contemplate until one is*
> *overwhelmed with the innate call to sense the presence of God*
> *To be, to become, to journey to eternity.*
>
> *I can only imagine about the fruit of this invitation*
> *participated in rightly.*
> *Imagine the sense of radiating warmth and power*
> *as one grows in this real closeness.*
>
> *The wonderful mysteries of life*
> *break upon one's dropping spirit*
> *like the rising sun over a long, cold night.*
>
> *The sense of wonder, the sense of urgency,*
> *the excitement of life!*
> *These are his gifts to us.*

On to living as a priestly man entrusted with the mission
to establish the Kingdom of God now!
His continued birth.
Our new birth into deeper life and greater love!
His life and His love!

Seminarian Immersion in Life of the Poor

Fr. Brian agrees with Pope Francis that we must move "beyond the image of a Church rigidly divided into leaders and followers," that priests must walk with their people. In his Address to the Faithful on September 18, 2021, Pope Francis noted the above and that:

> *"We shepherds walk with our people, at times in front [to lead], at times in the middle [to encourage and preserve the smell of the flock], at times behind...since the people too have their own 'sense of smell'. They have a nose for finding new paths for the journey, or for finding the road when the way is lost."*

Starting with their time in the seminary, priests are immersed in a clerical culture which sets them apart from the rest of the world. This has both advantages and disadvantages. It is the Roman Catholic belief that priests share in the one priesthood of Christ by way of ontological differences that are brought about by ordination and the power to transubstantiate bread and wine into the Body and Blood of Christ (Vatican II). The laws of celibacy, of course, set them apart, and most priests continue to live in a protected world free from many of the cares and responsibilities of the everyday man. (Refer to "Clerical Culture Among Roman Catholic Diocesan Clergy" – Voice of the Faithful 2011).

Once priests come into a parish, with its specific organization and ministries, it becomes necessary to adapt to the routine, probably making some personal modifications along the way. But there is rarely time to do an in-depth study of other needs, such as starting a program to administer to the poor in the nearest urban center, as suggested by Fr. Brian.

Bearing this in mind, Fr. Brian felt it was important to have programs where seminarians could be immersed in the environments where their poorest people lived, before they became responsible as parish priests. With this background, seminarians could "Involve, Rethink, and Reorganize" and take their learning with them when they were assigned to a parish.

In the mid-eighties, Fr. Brian arranged for eight seminarians to spend a week living with him in Trenton and working on renovating houses with and for the poor. Another year he brought in seminarians to help with programs in the Learning Center.

Seminarians on the streets of Trenton in
the 1980's

One of these seminarians, Fr. Bill Lago, recalls working in the after-school and GED programs. When he became the Catholic chaplain at The College of New Jersey, he felt drawn to passing on to his students the experience of working in the inner-city. He organized a volunteer program where his students provided various special classes for the after-school children. The classes, and the bonds formed between the after-school students and the college students, were unique and impactful. It is difficult to say who received the greatest benefit in this program.

For various reasons, the seminarian immersion program was not carried on, but Fr. Brian continues to believe that it is necessary that our future priests spend time living with the poor and developing experimental systems.

In 2021 Fr. Brian became aware of what was called an "experiencial" program for seminarians taking place in Yakima, Washington under Bishop Joseph Tyson. Fr. Brian saw this as a living example for having seminarians experience and understand the lives of their future parishioners and to put that understanding into action.

In this program, the seminarians found ways to bring their faith directly to seasonal workers and their families in the fields – including Mass, reading instruction, and food programs. (Seminarian Immersion Program Yields a Harvest of Pastoral Experience By John Gehring: National Catholic Reporter, September 17-30, 2021)

Bishop Tyson requires each seminarian in his diocese to experience a summer in the fields working and living with migrant workers. The article says that the program required a "shift in thinking about Church" and that "the idea for a migrant ministry began to develop in 2011 after Tyson asked the vicar for clergy in his diocese to identify the biggest challenge in vocations. The response was a 'sense of entitlement' among some seminarians who seemed more attuned to their own clerical status and institutional privileges than pastoral care… We wanted a more robust real-life experience for seminarians," the bishop said. "In the church of the past you had people coming to Mass out of habit. The church of the future is people don't come to us, we go to them."

It seems clear that many worthy church programs could be developed based on real-life immersion by seminarians. But, in order to carry out such immersion programs it is essential that there is financial support. The Yakima Diocese is fortunate to have received funding from the Catholic Extension in Chicago, a non-profit fund-raising organization that builds up Catholic Faith Communities in America's poorest regions. Funding is a key issue for programs like this and calls for creativity and generosity from those who see the importance of this kind of program.

In 2021, Fr. Brian wrote to the bishop and all the priests of the Diocese of Trenton telling them of the experiencial ministry in Washington and calling on them to create new tools for dealing with poverty in their own diocese:

"I believe it is our call to create, in the Lord, new tools for dealing with poverty and alienation and to constantly examine the way our Church addresses these issues. We need to thoughtfully design experimental and experiencial ministries to make this happen... I can't help but wonder how we should be addressing [these ills] today in our society, specifically, in our own poor urban or rural areas. Is now the time for a new experimental and experiencial ministry in our Diocese?"

PART IV – THE LEGACY

Chapter 9: Carrying On

By 2004, Fr. Brian was in his 60's, and the programs of Martin House were still going strong. The Board of Directors thought it was time to think about the future. They reasoned that hiring a CEO would both take pressure off Fr. Brian, as well as ensure that someone would be at the helm to steer them into the future. Systems needed to be documented and computerized in order to keep the programs ongoing, and innovative ideas were needed to guarantee the future.

Thus began a time of some upheaval for Martin House. It was difficult for Fr. Brian to define for others exactly what he did and to deliver control to someone else. In truth, his faith and strength of personality were the driving forces of Martin House, particularly his method of bringing tradesmen and volunteers into thinking it was the right thing to donate and discount their products and services. Bringing in these lower costs was what really differentiates BCHT from the now well-known model of Habitat for Humanity. BCHT was still the only program offering truly affordable housing to those under 40% median income. But without Fr. Brian, how could that continue? And how could Brian's message of Oneness be carried on?

The Martin House Learning Center also played a big part in the community. It was an anchor point, providing a preschool, after-school program, summer camp, scouting programs, and GED and ESL classes, as well as basketball leagues for people of all ages.

With Fr. Brian's retirement imminent, the bishop and Fr. Brian wrote letters to the priests of the diocese asking for someone to come in and head the Martin House Family of Programs, but that became a waiting game, and there was no move to look further than the priests of the Trenton diocese.

By 2012, two different CEOs had passed through Martin House, and Fr. Brian reached the retirement age of 72. Since no priest had volunteered to take Fr. Brian's place, the diocese felt it could no longer be responsible for insuring Martin House and funding it for $200,000 a year. (This was also supplemented with Fr. Brian's salary, which covered the directorship of the organization.)

The diocese asked Fr. Brian to step down, and it withdrew its funding for Martin House, effectively closing the program. It transferred the Learning Center building to the thriving Mercer County Catholic Youth Organization (CYO) and left the other "Twin Towers" building to Better Community Housing of Trenton, whose separate charter allowed them to continue as an independent charitable organization. Doorway to Hope, the Martin House program that housed and educated single mothers and their children, also became a separate entity, but it finally closed in 2018 due to funding changes in city and state structure.

After the retirement of Fr. Brian, Better Community Housing of Trenton continued on in a more limited fashion under the leadership of Pearleen Waters, who stepped in as Executive Director. The Board of Trustees kept her on at a similar salary as she had been paid as Fr. Brian's administrative assistant. They rely on donations and grants to carry BCHT forward. Pearleen now has the assistance of a part-time bookkeeper and a dedicated team of volunteers.

Social Justice in the Church

I asked Fr. Brian what he hoped his legacy would be, and in particular how well he thought the Church was doing with regard to helping the laity recognize the need to bring the world together as one people, to conduct their lives in a way that includes the poor and fights a society of Haves and Have Nots.

Fr. Brian said he is pleased that Better Community Housing of Trenton continues to provide housing for the very poor in Trenton, but that he is disappointed that the Diocese of Trenton no longer supports BCHT or other Martin House programs that have fallen by the wayside. He sees this lack of support as a hindrance to Oneness. He hopes that the Church and its people have recognized the COVID pandemic as a wake-up call that shows everyone how inter-connected we all are on this earth. All people, rich and poor, are linked by having to deal with the consequences of COVID. Fr. Brian feels that this is a critical time for the Church to redefine its role in making an equitable world. He said:

"I think maybe God wants me to use the message of Oneness to bring pastors to the recognition that all parishes must work to combat the poverty in their nearest urban [or rural] center, to bring home the Church's responsibility to foster Oneness."

Fr. Brian said he is encouraged by the 2021 Synod on Synodality movement promoted by Pope Francis, which was organized to bring change by addressing perceived issues in the Church at the parish level, which would then be synthesized at the level of the diocese, and finally for each country or region of the world.

The Synodal theme of *Communion, Participation, and Mission* is timely for our Church today. Fr. Brian is impressed by what Pope Francis said in his opening address about listening to the Holy Spirit as we journey together, leaving behind ideas that hold us back, and embracing the needs of the poor.

In his opening address, Francis said we must address the "emerging problem of how to organize the growing number of Christians, and particularly how to provide for the needs of the poor."

> *"You may say to me: '... Are the poor, the beggars, young drug addicts, all those people that society discards, part of the Synod too?' Yes, dear friends. It is not me who is saying this, but the Lord. They too are part of the Church, and you will not properly celebrate the Synod unless you somehow make them part of it or spend time with them, not only listening to what they have to say, but also feeling what they feel, ...*

> *[And] "Unless we include the "problem people" of society, those left out, we will never be able to deal with our own problems."* (Opening Address-Synod on September 18, 2021)

The Synod will not provide all the answers to what the Church's role should be in conscience formation and social justice issues, but let us hope that it will be a stepping stone and a basis for change. A major step for the Church would be better communication. Results from the National Synthesis show that the laity at the parish level sees a need in the areas of communication and social teaching:

- Communication between dioceses and parishes and parishioners that "could lead to Ongoing Formation for Mission."
- Conscience formation and social teaching: "social teaching is...our Church's best-kept secret." (Social Mission of the Church, Page 10 - *National Synthesis of the People of God in the United States of America for the Diocesan Phase of the 2021-2023 Synod)*

Perhaps the Synod will be the catalyst for introducing other more focused studies and responses to the issues that were identified in the first phase. Besides the top-of-mind issues like clerical abuse, celibacy, and closing of schools and churches, there were other issues identified as needing dialogue, including lack of inclusiveness (single or divorced people, LGBTG+, women in the Church, immigrants). This could be parlayed into Fr. Brian's take on "the Oneness of our inter-related society."

Controversy as a Facilitator

Fr. Brian's ideas and philosophy on social justice were often conveyed in ways that seemed extreme and confrontational to the bishops and some of Fr. Brian's confreres in the ministry. His approach was, and still is, considered radical by many – possibly even socialistic or communistic. In fact, at a meeting between Fr. Brian and the bishop in 1990, the bishop asked Fr. Brian if he thought he might be "slipping into socialism."

Though controversial, Fr. Brian's works and philosophy have been admired and applauded by many. Sister Eleanor Maragliano of the Catholic Commission on Urban Ministry in Newark said:

> Father Fr. Brian is a rarity. The established church is comfortable: they find it easy to collect money, send it and justify themselves that way. Father McCormick is like a John the Baptist crying in the wilderness, and because of that, other pastors don't always take to him. But if he were on an ego trip he'd have been deflated years ago. Look at where he lives [in the ghetto] – he doesn't have to be there. *Sunday Times Advertiser March 7, 1976*

The Times of Trenton commented on how Fr. Brian's outspokenness about racism and greed were uncomfortably challenging:

> **Priest Strives to Challenge Society** – *The Times of Trenton, June 8, 1998*

> McCormick's mission is not just to make a difference but to challenge society's institutions – including the church

– to get serious about social justice as a divine principle. His direct style and outspokenness about the evils of racism and greed can make some people uncomfortable. But it can also nudge them to act.

Fr. Brian's ideas differ from the norm. But let us remember that Pope Francis encourages us to see and confront differences of opinion. In his opening address for the 2021 Synod on Synodality, Francis said:

> *"[During the time of 'Acts'] there was also the clash of differing visions and expectations. We need not be afraid when the same thing happens today. Arguments are a sign of ... openness to the Spirit... Today too, there can be a rigid way of looking at things, one that restricts God's makrothymía, his patient, profound, broad and farsighted way of seeing things. God sees into the distance; God is not in a hurry."*

How we approach differences of opinion is key to gaining answers and promoting those answers to others. Fr. Brian would be the first to say that his ideas on addressing societal problems need to be discussed as part of an ongoing journey and dialogue.

If you have reached this point in reading this book, I hope you have gained a sense of how the persistence and faith of one person can truly make a difference. Individuals are important as leaders and exemplars, but to truly make a difference they must be part of an organized holistic movement that can gather many to work and journey together, to understand that "we are the world.".

Fr. Brian will tell you that the Church, led by the Holy Spirit, must take a leading role in the journey to form a just society.

So, how do we bring about recognition of the Oneness of society and the responsibility that places on the Church and every individual in our society? Addressing and promoting social justice, in general, is not an easy task. Even accomplished journalists like David Brooks have difficulty seeing how this can be done. In his March 18, 2021 NY Times article, "A Christian Vision of Social Justice", he speaks of this.

> "Like a lot of people, I've tried to envision a way to promote social change that doesn't reduce people to simplistic labels, that is more about a positive agenda to redistribute power to the marginalized than it is about simply blotting out the unworthy... and failed. [But] this week I interviewed Esau McCaulley, a New Testament professor at Wheaton College. He described a distinctly Christian vision of social justice [that] begins with respect for the equal dignity of each person. It is based on the idea that we are all made in the image of God. It abhors any attempt to dehumanize anybody on any front. We may be unjustly divided in a zillion ways, but a fundamental human solidarity in being part of the same creation.

> "...From Frederick Douglass and Howard Thurman to Martin Luther King Jr. on down, the Christian social justice movement has relentlessly exposed evil by forcing it face to face with Christological good. The marches, the

sit-ins, the nonviolence. 'You can't get to just ends with unjust means,' McCaulley told me. 'The ethic of Jesus is as important as the ends of liberation.' [The Christian social justice vision tells us that] new life is always possible, for the person and the nation."

www.nytimes.com/2021/03/18/opinion/social-justice-christianity.html

Arguably, social justice does not rely completely on Christianity, but it certainly makes sense to justify it based on Christian beliefs and to spread its word through a widespread institution such as the Christian Church. In Fr. Brian's words, there needs to be a "groundswell" that recognizes and addresses the serious lacks in our society. Perhaps we could look toward the young people in our colleges and universities, who are often idealistic and looking for a cause. Specific programs or classes could be created to promote and discuss these issues – possibly starting with the study guide at the end of this book.

In fact, there is a small seed taking root in the Trenton Diocese to raise awareness of the interrelatedness and Oneness of Society. As of this writing it is still just a seed, but perhaps we will look back and say, "Yes! This was sparked by Fr. Brian McCormick's ideas and work." A concert with the theme, "You Are the World," will include performances by groups from all over the Trenton area – city and suburb, rich and poor, religious and secular – all coming together to acknowledge and celebrate our interdependence. Performers will donate their time, and all proceeds will go to two charities that serve basic needs of the poor in Mercer County –

Better Community Housing of Trenton and Trenton Area Soup Kitchen. Music can be a powerful common ground that binds people together.

But I leave it up to you, reader, to contemplate and, perhaps act on, what comes next in our world's mutual journey to live together.

In his opening address at the Synod, Pope Frances reminds us that, by journeying together, we can bring forth a society that works together as one:

"We need to rediscover... [that] we are a people meant to walk together, with one another and with all humanity... we need to pass beyond the 3 or 4 percent that are closest to us, to broaden our range and to listen to others; at times they may insult or dismiss you, but we need to hear what they are thinking, without trying to impose our own concerns: let the Spirit speak to us."

So, we will wait and see what is next for the Church and the world. Let us pray that many will join the journey of communication, participation, and mission started by the Synod on Synodality, by listening to the Holy Spirit and acting on what is learned - possibly in some way hearing and heeding Fr. Brian's call for a sense of the Oneness of all of us here on this planet, earth.

PART V – MEDITATIONS ON LIFE AND FAITH

Meditations by Father Brian McCormick

The following meditations were written by Fr. Brian McCormick, mainly during the years of 1970 – 2012, while he was working at the experimental ministry of the Martin House. The ministry was set up in 1968 by the Priests' Council of the Diocese of Trenton, NJ to locally address changes the Church and the world were facing. Race riots were taking place all over the country, and, at the same time, the Church was just beginning to see a decline in priestly vocations. Martin House was to provide a new view of these problems to help the Diocese assess and address them. The priests would live among the poor and try to ascertain what role the Church should have in fighting poverty and racism, while putting that learning into practice.

Fr. Brian took this mission seriously and wrote many letters and meditations to the bishops, his fellow priests, and the people of the diocese to convey his learning. Sometimes he just wrote for himself, to clarify his thinking.

These writings are being shared here because they are insightful and thought-provoking. (Meditations shown in their entirety in the body of this book are not shown here.)

I. The Neighborhood

Fr. Brian encountered many people and situations, both good and bad, while he lived among the poor in Trenton.

OLIVIA, Noble Woman 1976

Fr. Brian wrote this poem to a dedicated helper from the neighborhood, who came to him and offered to help in any way he needed. She became an integral part of Martin House – Fr. Brian's organizer, typist, and touchstone for the neighborhood.

You feel so much the desperation of your race
You absorb so much the pain of your clan – (The family plan)
You become the sorrow of your race.
Deeply felt and loving accepted.
You bear this burden beneath your stony façade
of brick-built personality

Red brick	*All men*
	...especially black,

	...and father too, and brothers also,
	...are no good.
	...They are all seekers of the great get over.
Cement	*Yes, but I love them.*
	...I am willing to keep what we really have
	...Their pain is my pain
	...Their goodness is my goodness
	...Their dream, my dream
	...Their Godly destiny, my destiny
	...I will bear the burden.
	...For somehow I hear the call of God
	...and I cannot and I do not want to turn away.
The Cost	*One must realize – Brick buildings*
	...are heavy upon a stone foundation.

One must realize

*...she bears this burden
and carries that weight.*

Yet I believe

*that in her heart she hears the
spirit sing,*

*... "Someday, my love, you will
understand that*

*..."yes, indeed, brick is
drab-colored red*

*..."and is about as warm as
ice-covered lakes.*

... "But underneath,

..."I tend your woman's heart.

*..."You have heard the voice of
God,*

... "felt the pain of sorrow

*..."paid the price of loving,
self-sacrifice.*

*... "Let me whisper now in the
secret center*

..."of your most sacred self

..."what the union of your
faithful love means.

..."In the building of your life

..."I will let new songs of children
sing.

..."In the strongness of your center

..."I will protect, fragile and
frail,

..."but precious and true, dreams.

..."Within the beauty of your
straight lines

..."and the stability of your form,

..."I will have sons of the living
God leave you

..."to build new edifices of noble
grandeur."

Thank God

And so ends this little vision
with what it should really be,

a prayer – simple and to the
point. AMEN!

What's Happening at the Martin House *4/6/77*

Many of the people Fr. Brian dealt while living in the ghetto were very challenging. As briefly noted in Chapter 2, there was a neighbor, **Curtis**, to whom he repeatedly gave food. But Fr. Brian found out from the man's son that he had been selling the food to buy liquor. When the man approached him again, coming to his house and insisting, Fr. Brian worked through his anger with this meditation, not forgetting the goodness that also had a home in his neighborhood. This more inclusive version of the meditation recognizes both the good, **Little Bundle of Beauty,** and the challenging, **Curtis.**

Little Bundle of Beauty
The little girl rapped softly on the door and came in.
She put herself down upon the big worn couch.
Her very large eyes sparkled and stared.
They, looking lovely, shined out
from the lightness of her features.

She said, "Do you have a coloring book?"
"Sure," and I pointed to where they were.
She took the books and crayons too.
Set now was her purpose.
Off came her little coat.
Busily and happily she went to work.

Then the phone gave its command.
And I raced to answer its insistence.
A young boy, eleven, the little girl's older brother,

was on the phone. He said,
"Tell Curtis, I didn't tell you that he sold the food."

A few seconds later
Curtis comes limping across the street.
Bounding through the door
he thrust his whole person
into the middle of my home atmosphere.
"Hey, Father, you can't do this to me!
I need some food, and you're a Father
and you got to help me."

The little girl looks up.
She has seen this scene too often.
She, just a little while ago,
left her house to escape this exact situation.
She handles her problem the way she knows best.

The little bundle of beauty bundles up, and lifted
by a fine gentle breeze (a quiet call for peace),
slides softly and slowly off the couch and out the door,
unseen and unbeknown to the elements of chaos.

That little boy who just called, once said to me,
"I like coming to your house.
You bring nice people here!"
At that time my feeling part responded
to his unsaid observation:
"as opposed to the not-so-nice people who come to my house,"

I have always kept that communication in my heart.

Curtis
"Hey, Father. I need some food.
You're a father, and you have to help me,"
That little army in me wanted to go to war!

My army sees the truth of the situation.
It would be easier to destroy than to restore.
My army begins to murmur, "It isn't worth the effort."
Oh, that army is ready to march!

"Wonder-Counselor," my best part is screaming.
"God loves this man – Quickly, how does it fit in?"

Wonder-Counselor says,
"Remember my name is Truth.
All of you must live by the Truth."
"If you do,
He will find: real solutions and achievements.
Your army will always be alive.
The boy will find life and a home.
And God will be found in your midst."

I said, "Curtis, if you don't get out [of my house]
I just might throw you out."
My little interior army of rebels applauds –
I tell'em to shut up.
He leaves.

Alone,
I say to Wonder-Counselor,
"I'm Trusting in You. But it is hard to believe."
But underneath my self-pity,
deep underneath, I wink.
It is really not that hard to believe,
and I have an almost absolute confidence.
Fidelity is the greatest difficulty.

When Jesus Came to Earth 1/5/76

By two twelve-year-old girls, Dee Dee Mack and Jacqueline Sherman

The following meditation was written by two girls in Fr. Brian's bible study class, a class he started when several girls were upset that he had so many programs going for boys. They said, "You know, girls need 'Fathers', too." So, he started a Bible Study class just for girls. One of these girls, Jackie, kept up with Fr. Brian over the years. In 2021 she sent him a Christmas note. It said, "Just a few lines to let you know I appreciate you. You are just like a father to me, ever since I was little growing up, and you still are. I want to say thank you so dearly from my heart for all you have done for me and still doing for me. You are in my life for a reason. And I love you, Father. Thank you, Jesus, for the blessing you have given me. Merry Christmas, my blessed father."

The Meditation

One day Jesus came to earth. He came to the eight hundred block of East State Street.

I was hiding in the alley and this is what I saw. I saw Jesus standing there looking around, and there were no children outside.

All the children looked out the window. "Look at that man," they said. He was just standing there. They said, "Who could he be?"

So one of the kids went outside. And Jesus called him and asked, "What is your name?" He said, "My name is Tom." Tom said, "What is your name?" He said, "I am Jesus, the Son of God. Go tell your friends to come here and do not be afraid."

So Tom went to get his friends and he said, "Jesus wants to see you and do not be afraid of him." One of the kids said, "You got to be kidding, Tom." Tom said, "If you don't believe me, come see."

"I'll come. I'm not afraid," said Cheryl. So they went back to see Jesus. Jesus asked all of them their name except Tom. They all told him. Then they were no longer afraid of Jesus.

Jesus then said, "I am going to teach you the right way to live. You must listen to what I say if you are to learn. The proper way to learn is by the Ten Commandments. They are:" [Jesus recited the Ten Commandments.]

Then Jesus being very serious said, "Are you going to obey the Ten Commandments?"

Tommy then said, "I have a friend, Billy. He steals." Billy said, "I do not steal, Jesus. Tommy, if you are going to lie on me, I'm not your friend anymore."

Tommy said, "I was lying. He does not steal." Jesus said, "You are going to obey the Ten Commandments. Here you are already lying."

"Forgive me, Jesus."

Jesus said, "Why would you lie if you said you were going to obey the Ten Commandments?" Tommy said, "I didn't know you were serious."

Jesus said, "Do you lie to your mother and father when they have a serious look on their face?" Tommy replied, "I can't tell if my mother is serious or not because my mother smiles all the time."

Jesus said, "Come on. There is a time to be serious and a time to play."

Then Jennifer said, "Jesus, when are you going to stop talking?"

Jesus said, "How dare you be so rude to me?" Jennifer said, "I wasn't really talking to you, Jesus. I was talking to Tommy."

"Why would you use my name if you were talking to Tommy?" Jennifer said, "I did it by mistake."

Jesus said, "Don't do it again. You should not take the name of the Lord lightly. I'm angry. You play too much off. I have to go. When you decide not to play with me I'll be back."

Hampton Ave – "Come Out"

In this meditation, Fr. Brian anthropomorphizes one of the broken-down houses that BCHT is renovating, likening it to the broken-down spirit of one of its previous tenants.

Boarded box of disintegrated lives pops open
as I unwrap this hollowed thing with my crowbar and hammer.
Having positioned myself sturdily on missing porch
and having laid my hammer to positioned crowbar,
it moans out its ghostly language
through the disintegrated thoughts of a young man.

"Hey, man, I need a job!"
A truer statement a house never made.
Taken back, I stand back.
This is a haunted house!
There are many tales of woe that must be heard
before its chilling story can be understood and dealt with.

I crawl through the charred window
as it leaves its darkened stain on my white work pants.
"Hey, man, I need a job!"
It is the chained cry of the entombed spirit that
echoes through the charred windows, the falling ceilings,
the garbage-laden floors.
It ricochets off the doors, up the missing walls,
through the holey ceiling, out the roof.

There are many (Mark 5,9) ghoulish voices that speak this day.
For now, I am only after one (John 11,3).
My heart beats quickly (Mark 5,4) as I sense I am alone
within this haunted place,
pursuing an agonized and hostile spirit.

I hear his moan again.
"Hey, man, I need a job."

I shout out, "Imprisoned spirit, brother in pain,
where are you? Come out!"
"No, no. I will not get near you until I have a job."

"Pained brother, come out. Trust me."
"No, no. I trust no one. Only a job can call me forth."

"Friend, child of God, you must show yourself."
"No, no. You would know where I am.
You could get close, and you would hurt me!" (Mark 1, 23-24)

"Fragile brother, you must understand.
There is a God who loves you.
His son, Jesus, can make you stronger than all the pain.
He can give you a love that is worth all the hurt.
Do you believe this?" (John 11, 26; Matt 17, 7)
"No, no. Leave me alone. Let me
be among these emptied bottles on this broken chair,
to live my own life." (John 11, 37; Mark 5, 7)

"Brother, it doesn't have to be." (John 11, 40)
"It does!"

"You are important.
But for you to feel good, you must show yourself."
"Fool you are.
Never will I leave this place to show myself to you!" (Mark 5, 10)

In anger, the house shakes, dust whirls
till my own body looks as if it is coming through a cloud
from the nether world. (Mark 5, 5)

Anger and hammering. Anger and stomping.
"Never, never!"

I slide out the charred and broken window.
Through the whirled wind cloud, I shout out:
"I will be back, brother.
I need more spirit. (John 11, 6; Matt 17, 19-21)
I am going to the Lord of History,
and with my prayer and penance,
ask Him for the power to overcome this haunted place."

As my left foot hits the remaining part of the porch
I hop three steps to get my balance.
Steady on my feet, I look up.
A police car, symbolic of structured society,
comes slowly up the alley, to a halt.

They know me and our work. They slowly turn and pull away.
I think, as I rewrap the building with nailed plywood,
what would have happened if at that moment our hopeful voice
would have called forth the entombed and fragile spirit?

II. Christmas Meditations

Each year Fr. Brian wrote a Christmas letter to priests, donors, and friends. Some years he included his own meditations.

Christmas 1979 – Jesus is Our Guide

1979 was another year of crisis in the world. Tehran held 63 American hostages, the Three Mile Island nuclear plant was compromised, and the USSR declared war on Afghanistan. Amidst all this, Fr. Brian asked us to let Jesus help us recognize the interdependence of all and guide us to a new future.

The dramatic events of changing times
fill us with uncontrolled apprehension.
We are forced to take our first steps into the chaos.

We discover life goes on.
Fear is rather useless.
Withdrawal promises eventual violent confrontation.

Life demands that we live.
And living demands that the moments we spend be filled with
the sparkling jewels and the gleaming glitter of meaning.

More than ever
Jesus demands our attention.
The temporary illusion that our civilization alone
has control over our environment has faded
like the early morning mist
before the onslaught of the rising sun.

Illuminated before us is our total tiny globe with
its billions of people, its many cultures,
its varied nations, its interrelationships
and its interdependence.
It is a beautiful and terrifying sight.

All of this demands
a new comprehension, a new way of dealing.

Jesus promises to be our security,
our guide, our architect
to a wholly new future.

Christmas c.1981 – The Courts of the Worldly

This year, Fr. Brian realized that Better Community Housing of Trenton (BCHT) could not continue to build the houses for only $24,000, or continue to charge the new homeowners only $11,000. He was already asking much of the tradesmen in terms of their discounted time and goods. At the same time, some of the new homeowners were becoming proud and pointing out to the less fortunate how good and deserving they were – they deserved what they got and more! This raised the question – was BCHT producing what they were trying to counteract? How could they – and how SHOULD they – continue their mission?

Each year the star reappears.
Each year we sense we have spent too much time
in the courts of the worldly.

Each and every Christmas we are challenged to realize
it is to eternal life we must go.

Each and every Christmas the bright star,
the vision of our youth, reappears
to lead us to our glorious destiny.
Will we go?

Christmas is a call to journey out from worldly courts
to eternal life,
to reaffirm our destiny to be children of God.

This year we paused to consider how
our "miracle houses" were done.
When we reviewed the cost, when we studied the labor
we saw we were becoming satisfied
with staying in the courts of the worldly.
We were suffering from being too long in the gaudy, shallow,

and insensitive atmosphere of worldly allure.

Why are we alive?
We need the age-old star. We need the age-old answer –
Justice and vigor in Jesus' name.
We needed the vigor and courage of the journey, that is,
the discipline and sacrifice of self to find the real Messiah.

THE COURT – HEROD'S PALACE – OUR STOP-OVER
– OUR HOME?
[The homeowners:]
"We put in time." (But who did the meaningful labor?)
"We paid for it, only half price, and got credit, too."
In the Herod Halls of the vainly proud,
hollow exaggeration is ever echoed. LISTEN:
"Look how nice my house is."
"I only paid this much."
"I have a beautiful rec room."
"I did most of the work."
"Of course, we got a lot, but we should have gotten more."
"I deserve it, you know."

The non-journeying worldly – Herod's playmates –
are always trying
to say that what they have or who they are
is decisive and all important.
Vision, the star to be followed,
shows us that the Christ is most important.

And from this we realize the journey
from worldly courts to Him is truly decisive.
All else is hollow.
All wise men know this.
It is on to justice and to the journey of self-discipline,
personally applied.

We said the [house-building] cost - $24,000 –
cannot be accepted.
We must, through responsible, corporate, cooperative effort
lower the cost and raise the price from $11,000 to $12,000.
Otherwise, only the privileged few,
preferring to live in Herod's worldly courts
will get a decent shelter.

We cannot be so vain as to smugly say, "I paid $500 down
and $124.46 a month, so I deserve [a] $24,000 [house]."
We cannot be so self-satisfied that we feel our 200 hours
of unskilled labor deserves 1550 hours from other people.

From our homes, children of God with vision and energy,
must emerge, or the Christ in each of us will never be found.

Christmas 1983 – Seeking to Make a Difference

This Christmas Fr. Brian simply asked us to seek to make a difference.

CHRISTMAS
1983 of them

AMAZING:
Still, do we learn?

Are we willing to live so as to make a difference?
Or, do we just go along with what is
when the birth we celebrate
demands that we live for what we ought to be.

We ask that you join us
as we seek to make a difference.
We have and are making a difference.
We seek to do even more in Jesus' name
and with your help.

May the peace of men of good will be yours.

Christmas 1989 – A Thank You Carrying Startling Joy

In this year's Christmas letter Fr. Brian wrote about all that had been accomplished that year and thanked all the people who made that possible. Referring to this "thank you", he wrote:

It needs...
to ride on a welcomed breeze
to fall gently on an awakening spirit
to arrive with the new dawn's warming light

A "thank you" sincerely given
A "thank you" that carries
startling joy,

amazement, and admiration

The Christian adult depth of our Christmas efforts together was like the first Christmas Star that led believing doers to the infant Christ. I let the light of that star lead, and the wonder of the encountered infant invigorate. In this journey we discover in His name, the embryonic unity of all of us and our own real solidarity in Christ, through the ongoing present-fact mystery of His "life-death-continued-with-us-resurrected life." Jesus still lives, resurrected and redeeming us now.

Christmas 1990 – The Deeper Christmas Spirit

Fr. Brian wrote a letter to priests this year, speaking of how God and vocation fill a priest's aloneness at Christmas.

By myself, reality!
Imagine. No – recall, remember!
Focus on what you have already experienced
as a man and a priest.

Christmas' hectic pace sooner or later drops us alone
at some time and place,
In the depth of quiet solitude... alone by ourselves.

In our experience there is
the immediate panicked demonic call
To run, to do, to fill up one's time...
Even the false call to relax, to hide.

This is not God's grace-filled moment
for his most dedicated ones.
This moment, heard rightly, is an invitation
To be peaceful, to consider,
to contemplate until one is overwhelmed
with the innate call to sense the presence of God
as one who is secure and protected,
to hear and speak to him of real life,
to be, to become, to journey to eternity.

We not only believe this. It is the core of our life.
It is the center from which we radiate our witness.
I can only imagine about
the fruit of this invitation participated in rightly.

Imagine the sense of radiating warmth and power
as one grows in this real closeness.
Imagine the sense of conviction and confidence
that the Living God, in all his love is eliciting
from his beloved who are willing to establish
his redemptive loving plan.

In this real time and place of called-for solitude...
this free embrace of the mystery of God
in the sanctuary of our priestly heart,
one is urged on by the Spirit.

The wonderful mysteries of life
break upon one's dropping spirit

like the rising sun over a long, cold night.
The sense of wonder, the sense of urgency,
the excitement of life!

These are his gifts to us.
In this place and at this time
the quickened spirit can only think about...
how to be true, how to be pure, how to be creative,
how to do His will.

This is the creative act of becoming holy!
Away with the rhetoric, and contrived lifestyle
that masks unbelief.
Away with the indecisiveness and anger
that masks laziness.
Away with this false sense of acceptance, gentleness, and humility
that masks timidity and a lack of courage.

On to living as a priestly man entrusted with the mission
to establish the Kingdom of God now!
His continued birth.
Our new birth into deeper life and greater love!
His life and His love!

Christmas 1991 – Our Creative Best: New Building

The Christmas letter included a reflection on Martin House's new building, which housed priests, a clothing store, and meeting rooms for Martin House.

For many many, many years and times
Folks found it too hard to believe!
But God did send His Son!

And so it is true, life as it is
Can be faced and is worth living!
We believed in God's love when many said
(Suburban:) 'Nothing good can be done there.'
(Urban:) 'This is the way it is.'

After twenty years
this beautiful building
with its special life-giving activities does exist.

Thank you, GOD! Thank YOU.

This Christmas
may we continue 'to learn' to love one another
by giving back to God our creative best.

Christmas 1993 – A Bud Blooms: The New Learning Center

By 1993, Martin House was growing by leaps and bounds. The following is a reflection on building the new 8,000 square foot Martin House Learning Center:

Like a bud about to bloom
This cold site (sight)
is about to blossom!

Building the new Learning Center

Only with Christmas Hope
in the hearts of many
Only with God-fearing strength
in the limbs of all
do marvels of told yesterdays
continue to happen in our todays
to benefit the legends of
tomorrow!

May they say of us,
"Good and concerned people lived here!
They loved and served God
They loved and cared for their neighbor!"

Christmas 1994 – Our Own Twin Towers

Fr. Brian thought of the two Martin House buildings, the Learning Center and the Priests Residence/Clothing Store as his Twin Towers, representing the selflessness and good of the Martin House, opposed to the ostentation and greed of New York City's (then) Twin Towers. He said the Martin House buildings were "modest buildings with a true purpose," but said the perception

"Twin Towers" with cross window
shining from the gym on the left

was in the eye of the beholder. He always felt that the illuminated cross window of the gym in the Martin House Learning Center was a beacon for Christ in the neighborhood.

Blinded hearts, hardened hearts,
anxious hearts, busy hearts
See only what they look for (MT 13:11-16)

But for the being-purified
and perhaps the young, the old,
They in wonder co-create
and so behold what unfolds.

Twin Towers – Our Crib '94
is gift-giving God our best
and ourselves loved
not better than our neighbor.

Once done (our miracle towers completed)
the sacrilegious,
the pearl stompers (MT 7:68)
Accept it as there (theirs).

For those who will see,
it is another burning bush (Ex 3:31)
calling for gratitude,
fidelity, and creativity!

To hoist this pledged relationship
in the gifted soil of the 21ˢᵗ century
is the most privileged work
in all human history.

It is the sure path
the blessed promise
the clear vision
to individual love
human solidarity
and eternal life!

Beyond all excuses
God is always accessible
and His gift of our life
is always creatively worthwhile.

From the height of the cross
and the advantage of this last place

one discovers the nourishing fount
meaningful life eternally!

Christmas 1997 – Spirit of Martin House

A well-known local African-American painter, Thomas Malloy, painted this scene of Jesus overshadowing the people of the Wilbur section of Trenton, with the iconic water tower in the background. Called, *Spirit of Martin House*, it was commissioned by Katherine Cecere for Martin House in loving memory of her husband Michael.

The Holy Spirit overshadowed. (LK1, 35)
the Virgin Mary
She, singularly and uniquely,
became the Virginal Mother.

She giving life
(purely) with no hidden agendas
(purpose) dedicated herself totally,
wholeheartedly
to the promotion of this Life,
the Father's Son, JESUS,
and to all life
to be begotten
by the new Adam (1 Cor 15,22-28, Eph 4: 17:32)

The Spirit of Jesus overlooking the Wilbur
section of Trenton

He, not only born, but risen
and with a continued-with-the-world presence
'Gives' His life by His Spirit overshadowing us.
Yes! (Acts 10, 44-48)

Christmas 1998 – Caring for the Left-Out

This Christmas Fr. Brian talked about the priority of including the left-out in our lives.

Today's celebration
Is because of yesterday's.

Remember as priority
The Poor, the left out, the sinful alien!
Certainly with respect to
Caesar Augustus' plans for Rome or
Herod's magnificent Caesarea Philipi,
they are of no consequence.

History continues to be the same.
God creatively "thinks" and
more importantly,
lovingly acts differently.

The mind of God revealed at Christmas
is crystal clear.
How are the left-out included?

Christmas c.1999 – New Glories Entrusted to Us

This meditation asks us to leave behind our "plunder society," which is based on taking from others, and look toward the glories of Christmas – while always remembering that God gave us Jesus, the bravest man to be in creation to show us how to live. Fr. Brian wrote:

Dear Friend,

Each year I try to sense how I perceive God's dynamic presence in my life and in the life of the world. This year again and again I see the need for us Christians to see that we must bring His message and values to every part of our society. We need courage above all to do this. I share with you this meditation. I send to you above all, God's peace and joy in this season.

Christmas every year
gives birth to new glories entrusted to us.

Jesus, present today
asks us to see a new star
to leave stable employments

to hear new songs
to leave familiar surroundings.

Never have I seen as clearly as today
that Jesus is the answer to life.
Employment of plunder:
People dressed so nice
Professionals in proper suits.
Mechanics surrounded in all their macho.

All secure
in self-centered minds and mantles of legal rights
hear new songs
among the drudgery of heaped up lies
of proclaimed goodness done in security.

If we truly believe not only in God
but in His birth into our evils,
His birth is our birth into the vocation
of being God's power to bear the burden
to redirect our destructive direction.

There is no magic. There is only
Birth
Belief
Hope
And melodious songs to be heard
joyous sounds to be responded to.

The horrible day of the Cain event
ever so close to each of us
in our successful lives of plunder society
awaits each of us
if no songs are heard and no joyous sounds responded to.

Christmas is no pretty, pleasant story.
It is the event
by which our Father gave to the world
the bravest man to be in creation
to show us how to live.

Forgotten, trampled little folks:
For all who wake in the morning
stuck with being awake for a full day
with no way to escape that feeling
that nothing, absolutely nothing, really means anything.

For all, who being together with many others
raise the only star they have
the jive of hip street talk that leads busily nowhere.

For all, who hear the only song they have,
the tune of excitement
and the dance of hurting one another,
played on the big brown bag and the little white case.

The poverty family – Joseph and Mary
received the birth of their son.

They saw stars of grandeur
that gave light and comfort to every day.

Songs of great expectations played in their hearts
gave music to even the hardest of labors.
Never war's dreams of others' total destruction
Never Cain's giddy song to comparison and fratricide.

Christmas is no pretty, pleasant story.
It is the event
by which our Father gave to the world
the bravest man to be in creation
to show us how to live.

War:
with its power to totally annihilate
is the star that calls for all to seek a new direction.

If we truly believe not only in God
but in His birth into our evils,
His birth is our birth
into the vocation of being God's power
to bear the burden
to redirect our destructive direction.

There is no magic.
There is only
Birth
Belief

Hope
and the glorious star to be seen,
the glorious star to be followed.

The horrible day of fire, of storm without a Noah's Arc
awaits our race
if no followed-star leads our lives.

Christmas is no pretty, pleasant story.
It is the event
by which our Father gave to the world
the bravest man to be in our creation
to show us how to live.

Real belief in Christmas
calls on us to be as brave as he was.
With His courage
we as individuals
and as a race
have a future.

May His Birth
find its place in our hearts.

III. Miscellaneous Meditations

Faith/Responsibility 1977

Fr. Brian wrote this meditation, Faith/Responsibility, in 1977 as he thought back over the years he had spent in seminary, in his first assignment in Woodbridge, NJ, and his early years at the Martin House, when he was trying to come to terms with what was expected of him and what he felt, in his heart, needed doing. As editor, I have taken the liberty to break this meditation down into three separate parts, with the fourth and last part, Peniel, appearing in the body of the book in a section called: Interlude.

Faith
In faith I believe
the Lord has sent me
on an important mission!

I race home from a weekend assignment.
Calls to be made, people to be moved.
I run into my first roadblock,

a psychological wall of disapproval.

It is my feeling
that if I call people in this priest's parish
He will feel, though,
if I said it to his face beforehand
he would deny it,
that I was sneaking around in his parish.
I also know that he said he would get back to me
about attending a May meeting at his parish council.

It's June.
When I call to tell him I'm calling for volunteers
under our agreed-upon relationship
he will be uptight about the May meeting.

Our clerical culture would suggest – procrastinate!
Faith and responsibility call for action.
I will offer my faith and responsibility
for which I will gain greater distance.

I call, I get the associate pastor.
I express what I am going to do.
I feel the distance.
I sense his unwillingness to deal.
So be it.

l call, and I call, and I call their people
hoping to offer them a chance

in the Salvific mystery of the redemptive Christ.

It's my energy.
It's my time.
It's my money.
It's my Sunday night
trying to build possibilities for the people of God.

Christ is Here
Am I wrong? Ls it an illusion
to envision Christ redemptively involved in the city,
rejected as one who has no comeliness,
to envision Christ there
because those surrounding him have placed Him there?
How – in secret meetings,
taking what was best from Him;
in public proclamation,
downed Him for his lack of progress
and lack of care of what he had;

To envision Christ here!
As one surrounded by
an ignorant mass
listening to the lies
and hearing only those things that feed into
their fearful and impotent lives.

That mass that Christ saw from the cross
as they stood there in their

lies
fears
impotency
and illusion.
As witnesses to the death
of an evil man
pointed out to them so well by their leaders.

Christ saw them and said:
"Father, forgive them
for they do not know what they are doing."

My Reality, My Faith
The mystery of iniquity goes on!
"Listen, Fr. Brian: You have done much
but your tactics are a problem to me.
"You say your approach is the best approach.
"Look at the results.
"I suggest you look into your approach."

Maybe
my fellow priests are right –
They say, "Many priests and pastors
are interested in our cities...
priests who are vitally interested in social questions
and how the Church can best meet the need of our people."

My head spins and spins.
I like the priests, the statements.

All are correct.
But my feeling is
there is no reality behind any of this.
It's nice guys ~
living behind a façade of safe and secure,
wishful and wistful slogans!
Their lives
their message
their organizations
carry no power to achieve anything!

Lord, am I right?
I'm tired -
why not just go along
with this organizational tide of pleasant illusion.

Lord, is there a faith
that points out faithfully
what I am called upon to respond to?
Your faith
Gives me the ability to respond
to what in faith you show me.
To that vision I will be responsible.

But Lord, I'm only one!
So many say what is being said,
"Your tactics, your approach."
Lord, is the situation so serious
it demands top priority ~ now?

Is the involvement of our people so great
not only must they immediately recognize their complicity
but make significant amends by positive action?

I believe it's true, Lord!
Am I right? Am I right? Am I right?

Who will answer – should priests vote,
then we will know?
Is there a discerner of wisdom
who will tell me,
then I will be enlightened?

But I can't trust conventional wisdom
wrapped as it is in the symbols and illusions
of this society's successful life.
Will voices come from heaven
to announce God's providence,
Christ's redemptive act,
As it remakes creation today?

Lord, the conventional signs of one who is searching,
who is open,
are not with me.
Lord, I've been full of Faith
too long –
Lord, through your power I've been responsible
too long
If I were to say I'm in doubt,

I would be a liar.
I know, Lord, you want the force of your message here!

-

It bothers me, Lord.
It bothers me, Lord.
It bothers me, Lord.

The Christian Troublemaker c. 1978

This is a meditation of contrasts and contradictions - and questions about what the visible really means.

"But he spoke this parable also to some who trusted in themselves
as being just and despised others." Luke 18,9

It seems to me to be very possible
that the maker of trouble
is the bringer of Christ.

Jesus walked the lonely and dull night.
He saw boys and men drunk and drugged and violent.
This was trouble.

Jesus wandered the same crowded and confused place by day.
He saw many people, a community not seeing, not hearing,
not feeling,
a community well set
with no trouble.

Jesus visited the dull and dirty room.
He sat and smelled the atmosphere
of the frightened, the forgotten, the isolated.
This was trouble.

Jesus stopped at the dull and dirty place.
All the good people call it atmosphere
though most just sit, and the place smells.
Their isolation and confusion are absorbed.
But it is an orderly place
this club, this bar, this organization.

Jesus was present at the sacred meeting.
Everybody knew everything.
All were uptight.
They hated each other

But hated their chosen enemy more.

Resurrected Life (In Us) c.1988

BCHT gathered the people together on a regular basis to conduct neighborhood cleanups. Fr. Brian wrote this around 1988 after a community cleanup that removed loads of trash from the neighborhood. He wrote it as an explanation that "the good things we do" are based on Christ's resurrected life in us.

Our Witness – Our Reason Why
We Live Our Belief
Not Just In Church But In The World

The mystery we hold to be true
The mystery we live by today...Is:

God's son, Jesus, came from His perfect Heaven
to our God-given but humanly organized world.
His Father asked Him to love us.

He loved us strongly
but we chose to love our own ways more.
Our very self and our ways reject and crucify Him.
His pure love crushed,
has been raised by His Father,
now victorious, to new glorified life!

This pure love is passed to all who face the truth,
who dash to death their former life,
and faithfully and lovingly follow Him.

We know His strength and His Love
can and does change the worst evil.

We know His strength and His Love makes us so strong that
we don't go into evil, and don't give up.

This is the secret of the good things we do.
And it is freely available to the believing brave.

Squeaky Little Mouse – 1975

Fr. Brian had very strong and controversial ideas. He often came across as hostile or judgmental to his fellow priests. He wrote this in rebuttal to the response he got from priests to something he had written, which is now unknown. He made this dedication: *Dedicated to all priests who were shook up at a particular news article.*

There was a squeaky little mouse
who went to church every day
He wore a clerical shirt
and a clerical collar
And he spoke in a squeaky little way

He spoke much of the martyrs of old
but never said much
of God's need for bold martyrs for today

I now see why
squeaky little mice
want to build big stone churches
instead of keeping little squeaky ones

They want to get all dressed up
in front of a lot of people
and make like they are like the building
Big and strong and bold

Squeaky little mice
are squeaky little mice

Unless the Lord build this house,
they build in vain.

The Night Without is the Storm Within

Sometime in the 1970's the Diocese of Trenton gave a workshop on racism and discrimination for priests. This meditation was part of the liturgy. The author is not given, but the style is Fr. Brian's, and a loose copy was found in his files. He believes he wrote it but cannot remember for sure. The meditation urges us to address the fear within ourselves and face reality. Fr. Brian is a man of strength – a man with strong passions and strong beliefs. He believes we all must work hard to overcome such things as fear, rage, and desire. One of his high school teammates described a time when their baseball team lost an important game. On the drive home Fr. Brian was so angry that he stopped the car at a spot close to the Raritan Bay and jumped into the freezing water.

Why do I fear the street, with its hostile unreality
and, here, with its blackness?
Why do I fear the street, with its violence
its drugs, its booze, its women
its confrontation, its pain?

A thousand well-meaning people

people just as afraid and as unreal
give a thousand well-reasoned answers
why a fearful person like myself should be afraid.

All those answers, all – not one
Never really answer the question
Why do I fear the street?

Fear and pain move over the whole place.
Knock 'em down, give me drugs, find me booze, let me love.
Where do I go?

A thousand calls for a thousand things.
Programs galore, people aplenty, talk mounting
The revolution of equal pain and equal harvest to the streets
The buoyant unconcerned smile of hope
with its hammer of despair.

Where do we go?
A thousand proclamations for a thousand things.

In this night
I hear thunder and I feel rain.
I see lightning and I see clouds.
As I hold my own
I know
(and if you want to call it belief, it's OK).
I know
there's a rainbow, and there's a sun.

And there is a tomorrow!

But more;
the rainbow and the sun are not enough.
The Spirit and the street hold the answer.
It's not the people,
it's not the problems, it's not the confusion.

These things do call for a response.
The real fear lies deep within oneself.
All the activity is like Adam and Eve
who in fear covered themselves up.

All these crazy calls from the street
call me from the sins I want
and to the consciousness I need.
Sins I want but can't have
Because they are not approved of by the position I hold,
and I hold the position I desire.

So many tons of impure motives.
How do we become real?
One understands
Only the real walk the streets without fear.
And only the Spirit has the fire
to burn us pure and make us real.

Come, Spirit, and move us to the street
that we may go

and every creature may know
there is good news to every problem
if only we are real.

The Priest – 7/2006

This is Fr. Brian's serious take on being a priest, written a few years before he retired from Martin House.

More than being there
more than being a person
that shares sorrow or joy;
or speaks words of consolation or hope
in intense human situations,
the priest
calls for a divine contact.

His "revelation" points out
that already our compassionate God
is mightily disposing all of creation to be
benevolent to all of us.

His word
calls all the listening children of God
to freely join in the united family effort
*to creatively create and build**
a loving history
resonating to tones of eternity.

God's real Priest echoes

*the call of Jesus, the ever-present Lord of History
whose Spirit empowers and makes possible all good.*

*God's real Priest
Offers only this worthy gift
in Jesus to the Father.
It is the joy of the 24 elders
casting their crowns to the ground
worthily! Rev 4, 10-11*

**Not the same as money-making status-approved success.*

STUDY GUIDE

The following questions are meant to provide a basis for discussion in classrooms, book clubs, and any gathering where people wish to provoke thought.

Chapter 1 - Formative Years

1. What do you think was most influential in forming the conscience and philosophy of Fr. Brian McCormick in his early years?

Chapter 2 - Revelations of an Experimental Ministry - Martin House

2. Involve, Rethink, Reorganize – is this a good adage for everyone as they live their lives? How involved should people get in what is going on around them?

3. Is our society in need of re-thinking and re-organizing?

4. The generational poor are poor both physically and mentally. Talk about the difference between the mental and physical states of poverty.

5. Can and should society help with both physical and mental poverty?

6. Comment on whether you feel unstable housing is a root cause of poverty and social problems such as joblessness and educational difficulties?

Chapter 3 - Creating an Unconventional Approach to Housing

7. What do you think of Fr. Brian's approach to low-income housing – getting construction and trade discounts, donations, volunteer help, and providing the financing instead of a bank?

8. Do you think the BCHT housing program helped change the "mental state" of poverty?

Chapter 4 - Relying on the Support of Bishop, Pastors, Lay Volunteers

9. Comment about the extent to which the Diocese of Trenton got involved with the ministries of Martin House and Better Community Housing of Trenton.

10. How important were deacons and volunteers to the success of these ministries?

Chapter 5 - The Realities of Low-Income Housing - Miracle Houses vs. Government-Sponsored Housing

11. Do government and business encourage greed in the building industry, as noted by Fr. Brian in his letter regarding the project North 25?

Chapter 6 - The Root of Poverty - Fr. Brian's Philosophy

12. Comment on Fr. Brian's idea that our society is based on greed. Explain the different aspects of greed that could affect society as a whole.

13. Do you think our society is set up to create a permanent underclass? Are we a society of Haves and Have Nots, with an ever-shrinking middle class?

14. Does our culture/society need to be changed in serious ways? How? How serious a problem do we have?

15. Should people in business be concerned about how their actions affect others? Would it be helpful for there to be an organization involved with the ethics of keeping costs down, preventing favoritism in choosing contractors or suppliers, etc.? What else?

16. Do you agree that people should tax themselves (and give to the poor) when they feel their business is gaining too much to the detriment of others?

17. What do you think of Pope Benedict XVI's comment on not letting economic choices cause disparities in the wealth of others?

Chapter 7 - Co-Creation

18. Fr. Brian believes each person is responsible for everyone – "You are not just you. You are the world." Does this mean we need to take responsibility to make the world a better place? Should the suburbs be responsible for helping in their nearest center of poverty?

19. It is Fr. Brian's belief that, with God, we co-create the world we live in and, hence, our place in eternity. He feels God reveals to us what we have created and who we are when we die. Can this be reconciled with traditional beliefs about heaven and hell?

Chapter 8 - Systemic Issues Require Church as Leader

20. Should organized religion be used as a means to promote changes in how society thinks and acts? Should the church be "the keeper of conscience"?

21. Is there a role that suburban churches could take in helping people see that we are all one? What do you think of Fr. Brian's five-step proposal for parishes to study and address the problem of racism/ inequality and poverty? What do you suggest?

22. What other institutions besides the Church could promote societal change? How do they relate to a lack of understanding of co-creation?

23. Do you agree with Fr. Brian's summary of issues that concern the laity?

24. What are your thoughts on whether there should be programs where Catholic seminarians can get involved directly with the people before being ordained as a priest?

Chapter 9 - The Legacy - Carrying On

25. One influential man, like Father Brian, can accomplish many things, but could it have been possible for his model to be captured so it could be carried on?

26. Assuming the changes are needed in the Church, is something like The Synod on Synodality a viable way to produce real change? What is lacking there? What other methods could be used besides a synod?

27. Fr. Brian McCormick has been called many things – a rebel, a troublemaker, a saint, a prophet, a visionary. How well does each of these descriptions work? How would you describe him?

28. Are the poor to blame for being in poverty? What part does the welfare system play in helping or hindering poverty?

29. Will poverty always be a part of society? How might it be lessened?

Part V. Meditations on Life and Faith

30. Comment on whether Olivia represents a typical woman of her race in terms of being the cement that holds together the

bricks of her family, while keeping God in her heart and hearing His voice. What else does this meditation tell us?

31. What does the meditation, *Curtis,* tell you about Fr. Brian's inner struggles as a man and a priest?

32. How does greed play into *The Courts of the Worldly*?

33. What does Fr. Brian mean in *New Glories Entrusted to Us* when he says, there is no magic, and when he states that Christmas is no pretty, pleasant story?

34. What do you think Fr. Brian is saying in *The Christian Troublemaker*?

35. Do you think *The Night Without is the Storm Within* is an accurate depiction of the feelings of many priests?

36. What meditation best depicts Fr. Brian's faith? How would you describe his faith?

ACKNOWLEDGEMENTS

Acknowledgements

Working on this book with Fr. Brian McCormick has been a labor of love. It was an adventure to go through his many writings and try to determine how to put them together into a cohesive and meaningful format. To help me figure that out I asked several people to read my drafts.

My thanks to Msgr. John Dermond and Msgr. Ronald Bacovin who urged me to define my goals for the book. Bob Dunne and Tom Baker also gave me valuable input on how to add clarity. The first title I had come up with, *Don't Shoot the Messenger*, focused the reader on how controversial father's works and writings were instead of zeroing in on an overall theme. Once I realized that the theme of "Oneness" guided everything Father did and said, it became much easier to create a cohesive book.

Pearleen Waters was invaluable in checking my information about events and people who should be included in the book. And I thank my husband Gary for reading many drafts and putting up with all the materials spread over our dining room for a whole year.

Without these people I would not have the confidence to publish this book. Thank you, all.

Linda Smythe Oliaro

August 1, 2023

ABOUT THE AUTHORS

 **Linda Smythe Oliaro** has always asked herself, "What is this world all about, and what is my place?" Linda majored in sociology at Montclair State University in NJ and went on to work for VISTA (Volunteers in Service to America) before settling into a career in market research. She likes to write to order and clarify things in her mind, and, in her career she enjoyed studying and writing about people's reactions to new consumer and pharmaceutical products. She has also spent considerable time formulating and writing grants for Fr. Brian McCormick's Martin House charities, for which she has volunteered for many years. She was thrilled when Fr. Brian asked her to put her organizing and writing skills to work creating a book that delves into so many subjects that interest her.

Fr. Brian McCormick was ordained a priest for the Diocese of Trenton, NJ in 1966. He was asked to join the experimental ministry of Martin House in Trenton in 1970 and stayed there, living with the underserved, until he retired in 2012. Martin House was formed to address racism and poverty, as well as the Church's role in this. Fr. Brian established many  impactful programs to help with housing, education, health/wellness, and self-sufficiency. He took his role seriously as doer and conveyor of ideas that brought to life the goals of his ministry of the Martin House. His hope is that this book will help religious and lay people understand and put into action what he learned about dealing with racism, poverty, and greed over his many years working in Trenton, NJ.